To Alice,
Thank you for the article and best of
success with Cherry Hill Neighbors!
(Neighbors)

RINGS

of

KINDNESS

D0770041

A Treasury of True
Heartwarming Stories of Kindness

May you always be blessed
with abundant kindness!

Matthew J. Goldberg

RINGS OF KINDNESS by Matthew J. Goldberg

Published by Matthew J. Goldberg

Copyright © 2023 Matthew J. Goldberg

matthewjgoldberg.com

Contact: matt@matthewjgoldberg.com.

Cover by Jennifer Givner, Acapella Book Cover Design.

978-0-9861132-2-2 (Paperback)

978-0-9861132-3-9 (Kindle)

To Robert J. Goldberg and Sara Passo Goldberg, my parents of loving memory, who set me on the path of appreciating and rendering everyday acts of kindness.

To all of you who elevate and inspire our world through your empathy for others, and your acts of kindness and love.

Table of Contents

Acknowledgments

My name shows as the lone author/curator/editor of this book, but I received a lot of support in the forms of story submissions, formatting and cover design, and overall encouragement.

In reverse categorical order, there are many people who encouraged me to follow through with this book, even during the times when I was discouraged by its lack of progress and my own inconsistent resolve to bring this concept to fruition. Whether some of them had a story to send me or not, hearing…sincerely…that this was a great idea—and that this is a much needed book for these times—was of great help to my sometimes-flagging morale. Thank you to all who lent me such moral support.

Thank you to Jennifer Givner, owner at Acapella Book Cover Design, for her spectacular cover design and stylish interior formatting touches. You executed those elements of my vision far better than I could have, and you were also a pleasure to work with.

A quick shout-out to my brother Josh Goldberg—a fine writer and top-notch editor—who I also consulted with.

While this may be obvious, in a book compilation in which I only wrote three of the 85 stories found within, I leaned quite heavily on our contributing writers. Please read a little more about each one of them in the (transparently titled) *Contributors' Bios* section. Others submitted stories that I could not fit into this edition, and I want to acknowledge their efforts as well. Thank you all for taking the time to not only think about this as a worthy book idea, but to also share a wonderful story that transformed this from a nice concept to (I daresay) a wonderful, uplifting book.

I would like to extend a special thank-you to Wendy Hammers, who not only contributed a beautiful story but also told a group of her writing students, colleagues and friends about this project. They may not have known who *Matt Goldberg* was, but your good name, sterling reputation and exquisite talents brought them into the *Rings of Kindness* community, and I am abundantly grateful.

Lastly but never *leastly*, it's not always easy to live with an uncompleted book that is primarily in your own head, and I'd like to thank my wife Ruby and son Benny for helping me to share that vision with them along the way. I hope that I treated everyone who contributed to this book with honesty, appreciation and kindness, as that was my intention. Yet, I know that sometimes those who we are closest to (often, our own families) live with a writer's (at least, *this* writer's) moodiness and periods of doubt. I hope that my kindness and appreciation extended to you as well, and please forgive me for the times that I may have fallen short of that.

And to all the people who continue to extend their kind hearts, words and acts to others with no strings attached, thank you for helping me see and be inspired by all the kindness that surrounds us.

Matthew J. Goldberg

Introduction

In the early days and weeks of the pandemic (two-and-half years ago, as I tap my keyboard) amidst the justifiable rising tides of fear which sometimes turned to panic, I was also struck by the high degree of selflessness and kindness that was evident in so many ways. Oh, we all read—and possibly experienced—people hoarding cases of hand sanitizer, toilet paper and other critical supplies, but concurrently, we also witnessed a proliferation of kind sentiments and selfless acts. This was apparent from news reports of health care and emergency workers attending to their patients with remarkable, indefatigable dedication. It was reinforced by my first-hand knowledge of friends and neighbors checking in on their friends and neighbors in their communities, expressing their deep, abiding concern with kindness and love. And it was further reinforced in so many life-affirming ways.

As a communicator, I was intrigued with this more optimistic perspective on these distressing, deeply challenging times. Despite our periods of isolation, it seems that we are now connected to one another like never before: not only by our viruses, but much more poignantly by our shared humanity. Our compassion. Our empathy. Our kindness.

And during those often troubling times, a little self-composed mantra somehow entered my consciousness. I found myself writing out or chanting the following: *See the kindness? Be the kindness. Spread the kindness!*

Frankly, this new mantra did not always come with magical powers—I'm still working on *that*—but it did remind me of the inherent goodness of people and my inherent belief that we are surrounded by kind people who are not only capable of kind acts, but who actually perform them daily.

This became a theme I wanted to explore in some way. How can I, perhaps how can we, *see the kindness, be the kindness and spread the kindness*? Several months later, in the fall of 2020, I was the recipient of an act of both terrific good fortune and kindness by a wonderful couple that lived just a stone's throw or so away. I wrote about it (with a tweak or two, it became my *A Ring of Kindness* story), and I posted it on a locality-driven Facebook page called *What's Up in Cherry Hill* (New Jersey).

This What's Up page is many things, but it's not primarily a site for writers. I simply wanted to post a nice, uplifting story with the premise that good people really do abound in our town…which of course, could apply to most towns. I posted it, and the response was overwhelmingly positive.

My post struck a most resonant chord, and one person commenting on it—who knew that I had previously written several books—suggested that the concept may be a good one for another book and… eventually… here we are.

It wasn't an instantaneous process for me to get firmly behind my own idea, nor for my eventual co-authors to respond to it. Life got in the way for over a year, but eventually, I committed to following through on what I hoped would result in an uplifting book that would acknowledge kindness and help (if in our own little way) spread it to the world.

Along the way, I didn't really feel the need or desire to define kindness. Indeed, if I asked each one of us for a quick synonym for *kindness*, I am sure that we would collectively come up with many different answers. Here are just a handful of synonyms found on thesaurus.com: benevolence; consideration; goodness; sympathy; thoughtfulness. Perhaps, I would add empathy to this list, and you might add...well...what comes to mind for you?

There are a lot of different ways to think about kindness, and various ways to express it in everyday life. If beauty is in the eye of the beholder, then it very well must follow that kindness is in the heart of the recipient.

One note: I asked each of our contributors to share a true story about a time when they received an act of kindness, but with this stipulation: I wanted the act of kindness to have been rendered by someone who was not a family member, a significant other or a close friend at that time. Much as I did not want to be The Kindness Police (I'm sorry if I may have bent this rule here and there), that was the dynamic that I wanted to capture and share with you.

As you will see from the stories presented in *Rings of Kindness*, kindness was regarded and acknowledged in a variety of ways and circumstances, settings and times throughout our lives. These acts of kindness—some seemingly small, and some quite heroic in nature—made a difference in the lives of all of the writers who were kind enough to share their stories. They took place in schools, subway stations and stadiums. During music concerts and during the horrors of The Holocaust. From Nova Scotia, Canada to Queensland, Australia.

These true stories made lasting impressions on us, whether we were looking back 60-plus years to a first-grade classroom, or they happened just days prior to drafting the story that is in this compilation. These moments of kindness resonated with the various contributing writers, and I hope that their stories will resonate with you.

As I started to receive these wonderful stories, I felt even more of a responsibility to include them in a book that each of us would be proud to be a part of. I hope that we achieved that, and further hope that you will enjoy and be uplifted by our stories.

I wish you a heartwarming read and the blessings of abundant kindness in your life.

Matthew J. Goldberg
Cherry Hill, NJ

ACT One

◊ ◊ ◊

See The Kindness?
Be The Kindness.
Spread The Kindness!

Matthew J. Goldberg

Fresh Flowers and Vintage Vases

In 2015, I was diagnosed with pancreatic cancer. (That's the cancer where, when people hear about it, they are so freaked out they actually say things like, "Oh. Isn't that the one that is supposed to kill you?")

I am *so* not kidding about this.

Anyway, this very cool woman who was *not* a close friend, but rather, a writing colleague that I really admired, left fresh flowers in a vintage crystal vase on the second floor doorstep of our Santa Monica apartment. The flowers were lovely, as was the vase, but what really blew me away was the act of sheer kindness. I was touched, moved to tears, strengthened by the gesture. I called to let her know that in the midst of medicine and tubes and painkillers, her gift of fresh flowers was just the salve I needed on the biggest wound I'd ever had in my five decades on the planet. This *owie* called pancreatic cancer.

"So unbelievably sweet for you to think of me, Sonya, but I've got to get your vase back to you."

"Yes, you do", said the voice on the other end of the phone. And then there was a pause...

"So I can refill it."

"What? What do you mean?"

"Well, my husband and I enjoy riding our bikes to the farmers market each week for flowers, and I love to collect cool old glassware from estate sales and use them as vases. If you leave the vase on the porch, we will refill it."

I was speechless. I barely knew this woman. Was it selfish of me to want more flowers? But I had already learned the first gift of cancer—let yourself receive. So, I did as I was told.

A few days later, I opened my front door to more fresh flowers, in the same darling container. The very next week, it happened again. And yet *again*. The flowers just kept coming. Each week, a variety of red, yellow, or multicolored daisies, tulips, daffodils, or wildflowers would magically appear in an equally beautiful jar or vase, filling our home with thoughtfulness and love.

Was this chick for real? Was she robbing a flower shop or frolicking through my neighbor's garden with cutting shears?

No, nothing that diabolical. Sonya and her husband were something even more radical—they were simply kind.

These flowers were vibrant and full of hope, which was just what I needed. Never knowing exactly when they might arrive filled me with anticipation and gratitude each time they did. This went on for nearly a year.

I am going to say that again in case you missed it. A *year*. I didn't know her and her husband all that well, but it was official—I was *in love* with both of them.

"How will I ever repay you?" I asked.

"It's simple", was her reply. "You will get better and do this for someone else".

And she was right. That is exactly what came to pass. Next month, I will celebrate seven years since I was diagnosed, and six years cancer free.

When I completed my treatment, my oncologist reviewed the scan, looked me in the eye and proclaimed, "Wendy, you're unremarkable".

"Unremarkable?"

"That is what we call it when the scan has *literally* nothing to remark on."

Who knew being called unremarkable would be the nicest thing anyone ever said to me.

I am crying as I write this. So grateful for my life and still in awe of fresh flowers on the doorstep, this ring of kindness that was put into play all those years ago.

My neighbor Julie is recovering from Covid, so just yesterday, I put a bunch of purple lisianthuses in a cut-glass vase and delivered them to her porch.

The tradition continues.

Wendy Hammers

A Walk in Someone Else's Shoes

For a long time, I was ashamed of my beginnings. It has taken spiritual growth to make peace with my story. I blocked out chunks of my life. However, I've never been able to forget a significant act of kindness from a stranger.

I was born into a family where domestic violence was normalized. Life was hell! We struggled to have food on the table. Our house had holes in the ceiling and sometimes it would get flooded. In those times, I thought my siblings and I would drown. We were alone most of the time and they were under my care.

As the oldest child of four, I had to carry the world on my shoulders at an early age. It didn't bother me. I took on that role with courage and strength. Looking back, I see that having a hard life was my training ground. I was always presented with the opportunity to step up as a leader, which has been one of my core values, an attitude and a habit. Filling in that role when nobody is stepping in to bring change is also, like Gandhi said, a chance to be the change you want to see in the world.

Born into poverty and fighting for survival every single day for years and years made me think for a long time that the whole world was like that. Living in Mexico, I observed that most of the males on both sides of my family were alcoholics who were uneducated and could be impulsive and angry.

Women were subjected to violence or coercive power if they were not submissive, obedient, and pleasing. However, even though there is a belief that women are the weaker sex, I saw women fight to survive with perseverance. They were resilient, and kept working hard for a better life.

Children were somehow treated as if they were invisible. The message was that adults have enough problems so don't even dare to bother them with anything. Our emotions were often seen as tantrums. Suffering was seen as a form of becoming tough enough to endure a hard life.

My siblings and I worked alongside my mom during our childhood. She would take work at home so all of us would help and earn some money to eat. She performed all kinds of jobs, usually two to three at the same time. It was difficult to advance because my alcoholic father would destroy everything we were trying to build. My mom would make our clothes out of discarded fabric from several factories around our area, and our shoes were made of plastic.

In a rough world where everything is about survival and hearts are hardened, a small act of kindness can really bring a renewed perspective. My perspective of the world started to change when a friend of mine from elementary school invited me to her house to do homework. I was in third grade. Even though my clothes and shoes were old, I was always clean, and my hair neatly braided. This was the first time in my life I saw a family take their hands around the table and pray. Their father prayed and I was astonished. I was invited to sit at that table, and they treated me like I was part of their family. Their kindness made me feel acknowledged, respected and honored.

Years passed, and I was fourteen years old when I tried to get a job in a house in downtown Mexico. A friend of mine had recommended me. I was timid when I rang the bell of the house. An older man who was an artist opened the door. He talked to me for a bit, showed me the paintings around his studio, and offered me water. We went out walking around the area where he lived. He suddenly stopped at a shoe store and asked me what shoes I liked. I was so embarrassed to tell him. After several attempts, I just pointed my finger at some dark green moccasins. *They must be outrageously expensive*, I thought. I stood there for a moment, and lowered my head to realize that my shoes were falling apart.

My siblings and I wore shoes that were always bought bigger than our feet so we could grow into them.

Our shoes were cut in front so our toes could have enough room until my mom was able to buy new ones. Some other times, the shoes had to pass from the oldest child to the younger one if they were still somehow in *good* condition. We would not get new shoes until the ones we had were completely falling apart or were unwearable. Until this day, I remember that man who bought me the most comfortable moccasins in the world. His kindness touched my heart deeply.

My feet had been cold, uncomfortable, and at times in pain full of blisters from wearing big shoes, no shoes, or ripped off shoes. However, that is not what I choose to remember. What always comes to mind is the gesture of this stranger who bought me shoes and that made a huge impact on my life. His act served as a metaphor that even when in the darkness, someone can light up your path as you continue walking. The kindness of this stranger made me feel that I mattered – that I was deserving and loved.

In Mexico we have a proverb that says, "Haz el bien, sin mirar a quién." It translates to "Do what is right, come what may." Walking in someone's shoes is compassion, understanding and love. It is to open all our senses to someone else's experience to change their experience through our words or acts. We see the world as we are and through the eyes of our own experience until someone comes and changes our paradigm.

My paradigm was changed, and that sole act of kindness from someone is a constant energy acting upon me. The whole world has changed because many humans have paid forward a simple act of kindness they have experienced from someone else. An act of kindness doesn't have to be something huge. It only has to come from the heart, and every day we have an opportunity to be a beacon of light for others.

Luz Sanchez

The Missing Key to an Unlikely Door

I waded in an ocean of bewildering thoughts about what plagued my fifty-eight-year-old sister. She became brittle, then, cracked. In a frantic race against time, I watched a loving vibrant woman transform into a grotesque, odorous, illogical, frail, homeless person.

Always a character that moved to her own beat, years of resistance shrouded in secrecy to signs of life's hiccups left questions for mysterious changes unanswered. After Beryl found her husband dead on the living room floor, the unsteadiness of her grief took on a darker pathological hue. With no family nearby, life alone in Chicago gave Beryl distance to hide what she didn't want anyone who knew her to see. Although signs of problems were evident, she tried to mask them with plausible excuses. I worried that being alone helped conceal the profound changes in her life. It saddened me to think of my sister in bed all day drifting further into isolation. I didn't understand what she was hiding at the risk of becoming homeless, or dead.

That all changed when Beryl met a stranger in a city corner coffee shop. Conversations about grief over the death of loved ones brought these two characters together. An important pivot in the timeline of Beryl's deterioration happened when this kind person entered her life, and consequentially, mine. For different reasons, we were all gasping for air when this stranger unknowingly buoyed our sisterhood in a storm no one saw coming.

At first, Gregory had no idea what he'd taken on in this new friendship. It didn't take long to get tangled up in Beryl's foolhardiness. As her appearance morphed into a creepy cartoonish version of herself, a cascade of problems poured out of every crevice of her world. Beryl's fierce denial sabotaged my desperate efforts to help her. With the uncertainty of my sister's path to personal destruction, a jittery pulse of fear thumped against every fiber of my being. I could only imagine what this man thought. After all, it was like he just showed up in the middle of a sentence with no context for all the chapters that led to this place on the page.

I wasn't sure what to make of this odd *Harold and Maude* kind of relationship. Born several decades apart, the older Jewish white woman from the burbs and the younger black man from Chicago's inner-city seemed an unlikely pairing. She enjoyed the security of a loving, stable home. He had the experience of a loving single mother faced with hardship and the protection of a shelter during his youth.

Somehow, this duo forged a meaningful relationship that included a craving for fun and a good story.

Even though I was suspicious of his intentions, I desperately needed to change the soundtrack playing in my head. How could he tolerate that rancid smell and fluid draining from her nose and mouth? Did he ignore the grossness because of a desire to take advantage of my sister's reckless vulnerability? I decided to follow my gut and a prayer for a ripple effect of Gregory's *boots on the ground* presence. With the first mention of this strange encounter, I felt the endless worry triggered by the thought of losing contact with my fragile sister begin to fade. And with a need for an explanation and fix to this baffling mess, Gregory could be instrumental in getting my sister to walk through the doors of an emergency room.

Given what was happening to my sister's life, the circumstances around this friendship seemed to fit like a missing key to an unlikely door. Although I didn't trust or understand this person, I trusted a stranger more than my own sister. The lift in her voice when relaying stories about her new friend was a relief, too. With a baseline of needs leaning towards shelter and food, knowing someone had an eye on Beryl gave me a reprieve to catch my breath before the next crisis.

While my sister's tattered appearance bordered on freakish, the last vestiges of her curated sexy vibe bolstered by a well-coifed hairdo, manicured nails, and ahead of the trend vintage finds, left Gregory with no idea how far his new friend had drifted from her brand of normal. I suspected Beryl tried to control the narrative, hoping he'd help her stay in Chicago.

Their friendship grew from invitations to dinner with Gregory's friends to living together to help with money problems. Slivers of familiar sounds of joy punctuated in the upbeat pitch of her voice were a welcome change to the tick of the clock pulling her farther away. Unknown to Gregory, his help also bought my sister more time to prolong dealing with a move to Columbus. His presence gave space for some hope when reality felt like the constant hum of a stereo needle stuck in the groove of a scratch on the vinyl.

As Gregory waded deeper into the muck of my sister's life, despite her challenges, he tried to help her fulfill an impossible dream finding a job and housing. According to Beryl, Gregory agreed this was all she needed to happen to hold onto the threads of her life in Chicago. I worried about this guy enabling her without understanding the big picture. Did he naively expect logic to emerge from the illogical? How would he know her family was worried, and trying to get her through the doors of an emergency room and back to Columbus where they could better help?

It took a long time to realize maybe my sister wouldn't do the right thing because she couldn't. Crazy produced crazier. Depression slammed hope. Sluggishness limited work. Confusion buffered the truth. Paranoia masked reality. Mental illness made it all so deceptive.

Because Beryl put so much trust in this man, it was a matter of urgency that we connect and work together. The

challenge was finding Gregory. Beryl refused to share any personal information, except his name. But there were too many *Gregory Wilsons* in Chicago to narrow it down to the right guy.

It took months before I finally linked with Gregory. The day our father died, when I called Beryl to break the news, she put him on the phone. Knowing Beryl's mindset could suddenly shift, I couldn't lose precious seconds and risk she'd pull the phone away. I talked to him like our lives depended on it. In a hurried voice, I asked him to quickly whisper his phone number. *And* the person he knew was not her normal self.

From that day on, Gregory and I stayed in constant communication. Although he started to feel the load of dealing with the crazy with the dial turned up, he didn't walk away. Instead, Gregory Wilson stepped up with a promise to keep Beryl safe and get her to Columbus, *because, as a boy, his mother taught him right.* Later I learned his family didn't understand his relationship with Beryl, either.

Eventually, he packed her PT Cruiser with the remains of her life. A few months after he watched her return to the bosom of her family, the day came that I packed a suitcase with a black dress to wear to my sister's funeral. When I walked into the hospital room, I found an odd sense of comfort buried in the sadness of seeing my sister lying in a quiet stupor with tubes pumping life into her damaged body. Clean, white, bandaged hands restrained her to the bed rails for her protection, and mine.

I remembered a similar feeling of comfort when an unknown man appeared, like an angel.

Gregory became a lifeline to my sister's survival. He helped pull back the curtain on a frightening reality. Avoidance of healthcare, a fake-it-till-you-make it attitude and masking excuses for symptoms of a medical condition, unexpectedly landed her at death's door with a diagnosis of myxedema coma crisis, a very rare life-threatening form of an untreated hypothyroid that caused her body to decompensate.

In the end, treating the hypothyroid allowed her mind and body to regenerate in a healthy way. In the year following Beryl's recovery, I met Gregory for the first time, at Beryl's neighborhood hipster coffee shop in Columbus, Ohio, on a day off from her caregiving job. We spoke about her illness and the future. I thanked him for showing up when my sister's life hung on the raw edges of psychosis. What attracted him to the woman with the sad soul became a huge gesture of his humanity. He gave her quality of life. This stranger's kindness and help disrupted her in ways that filled our lungs with hope when everything seemed so hopeless.

Sheri S. Dollin

Loss

I can still see and feel the lustrous book in my mind. Its pages were glossy and with the hard cover that engulfed it, it contained more weight than one would imagine from such a lean volume. I thought it to be the most beautiful gift I'd ever received... It was. It still is.

Upon opening the magnificent tome, I was captivated by the words within. These were words and phrases that were beyond my comprehension, as I was not even six years old. However, I was mesmerized by both the title of the hardback and even more intoxicated that it had been given to me. It was truly mine, and to this day I've never been bestowed a more wondrous reward.

The benefactor of this most beautiful present was named Mrs. Hyman. I do not recall her first name. I'm not even certain that I was ever aware that she had a first name.

To yours truly, she was "Mrs. Hyman." Mrs. Hyman was my first grade teacher, and she was teaching me how to read.

Mrs. Hyman was, as I recall, a slightly heavyset young woman who smiled a lot. I liked her very much. She was the first teacher I'd ever had. I had been unceremoniously tossed out of kindergarten for crying for my mommy. No, really.

The name of the book Mrs. Hyman presented me with was "Bobby Bluegum Plays Father Christmas." This, despite the fact that I was Jewish. For all I know Mrs. Hyman may have been Jewish. It didn't matter. I loved the book.

I recall being terrified of doors as a child. I don't know why. Closed doors still disturb me. I'm not fearful of what lies beyond the doors, but that I'd be locked out and prevented from re-entering. Mrs. Hyman seemed to sense my fears although I never informed her of my *malady*.

"Bobby Bluegum Plays Father Christmas" is long gone. My father, a strange man, would literally sell all of our toys... No, really. I won't even go into that. All I do know is that Mrs. Hyman saw something in me that I still cannot understand, not even to this very second. It wasn't as if Mrs. Hyman had given books to the other students in my class, at least to my knowledge. One day, she just walked to my desk and handed me the wonderful manuscript.

Mrs. Hyman had written my name and then signed the book "Love, Mrs. Hyman." I had never before seen the word "love."

Many doors have opened and closed since the day that I was given "Bobby Bluegum Plays Father Christmas." I received that gracious gift from that absolutely wonderful woman long before hearts could be broken, long before I saw meanness and cruelty. On occasion, doors still frighten me.

I know this in my heart. When the time arrived for Mrs. Hyman to enter the most meaningful door of all, she was welcomed with open arms.

Scott Russell

The Score

I was born while my father was 100 feet under the North Atlantic in a Polaris submarine. He was honorably discharged from the Navy when I was four, but he might as well have still been thousands of miles away and deep in the ocean for as connected as I felt to him growing up. He left for work before I awoke in the morning and came home just in time for dinner, usually cranky. We kids tiptoed around his recliner at night, cautious not to interrupt his beloved baseball broadcasts on the RCA with the sensitive rabbit ears. Jump too hard on the shag carpet and the signal would be lost. Dad had a temper, and we all knew it was best to let him fall asleep, undisturbed, in his chair.

Dad never shared much about his life. We knew the teams he liked (the Wolfpack, the Redskins, the Braves) and the beer he drank (Pabst Blue Ribbon), but we knew little about his time in the service or the difficult childhood that may have been a reason for his enlistment just out of high school.

Time moved on and I moved away. For years, Dad was the Dad of *"Love Mom and Dad"* at the bottom of cards in *her* handwriting. He was the guy who answered the phone by simply saying *"Let me put your mom on the line."* It's not that I was keeping score or anything, but Mom was a player in my life and Dad really wasn't.

After Dad became a widower, he began to open up in calls, bridging the distance between us. He started sending his own cards. He Hallmarked the heck out of holidays and even made up his own, remembering the anniversary of the day I met my husband or the birthday of my dog. For two decades, I've been given the unexpected gift of getting to know my father, the man who was an enigma for the first three decades of my life.

During one of his visits from North Carolina, on a long traffic-filled ride from San Diego to my home in Los Angeles, we got to talking about his regrets and hopes. He admitted that he wished he'd been more involved in my life when he was a young father. He wished he'd stayed in the Navy longer. *"Is that why you always wear your Veteran's hat?"* I asked. *"I guess it is just one of the things in my life that I'm most proud of,"* said Dad.

I asked him if he had a bucket list. *"That's not something I've ever thought about,"* he said.

"Well, are there any places you'd like to visit? Any quests you want to accomplish in the years you have left?"

He pondered the question for a bit before saying he'd like to travel to Australia or maybe Ireland, one day.

And he said he'd like to visit all 30 Major League Baseball parks.

As a lifelong baseball fan, that dream of my dad's made sense, though it would be a big undertaking. At that point in his life, he'd only been to four. It might be difficult to get him to Australia, but the baseball dream, I could support.

We had gone to several Dodgers games together on his previous visits to Los Angeles. When I saw that the Angels were in town, we headed to Anaheim the next day. The box office link said prices ranged from $10 to $300 *"Well, the game is my treat,"* said my dad, as we inched along in the Southern California rush-hour gridlock. *"So we'll be sitting a little higher up and closer to that $10 area."*

Standing in the ticket line at Angel Stadium, Dad shared how he and some of his Sub Vet friends had recently gone to a Durham Bulls game. The Triple–A team was on a winning streak, and they'd purchased their tickets late for a Sold-Out game. Their only option was to sit on the grass-covered "Home Run Hill." While they were waiting to buy beers, a group of men in their early 20s joined the line behind them. Noticing the older men's matching Veteran caps, the young men thanked them for their service. Then one young man asked, *"Where are your seats?"* My father pointed at the grass beyond the outfield where kids were running between blankets. The young man whispered to his friends, then turned to my father and said, *"We'd like you to have our tickets."* And that is how three old sailors found themselves sitting behind home plate.

"I don't know that you can count on such good fortune today," I told my father as the afternoon sun cast an orange glow over Angel Stadium's Home Plate Gate, and we crept along in the queue, Dad wearing his Veteran hat as always. Just then, a man approached us and asked, *"Sir, were you in the military?"* My father beamed at the recognition, and the man thanked him for his service, then handed us two tickets for seats well above our price range.

With beers in hand and peanut shells at our feet, we witnessed Japanese phenom Shohei Ohtani hit his first Major League career home run on his first at bat as a Los Angeles Angel. I looked over at my dad, beaming as he checked ballpark #5 off his newly created bucket list, proud that his military service scored us great seats and that his daughter was there to witness it.

Suzanne Weerts

Thank You for Your Service

Early one autumn morning some years ago, I was in 30th Street Station in Philadelphia, waiting for my train to New York. It never arrived, there was a switching problem in the yard, but I digress—that's not the story.

30th Street Station is one of the grand old ladies of the long-gone Pennsylvania Railroad system. Its cavernous hall is outfitted with enormous high-backed wooden benches for its passengers' comfort—think of church pews with a glandular problem.

I took a seat on one of these at the end of a row of four young men bedecked in their flawless dress uniforms who were all headed to various destinations afar.

Presently, an elderly gentleman approached them and began thanking them in a very humble fashion for their service.

"I appreciate everything you do for us, and the sacrifices you make, and I just thought I should say *Thank you*".

The young men were taken aback. They glanced furtively at one another to silently elect a spokesman.

The curly-haired young man furthest from me spoke. "Thanks. We really appreciate your saying so. Most folks just walk by...but we're really just doing our job... thanks".

The gentleman continued, "I'd like to buy you each breakfast..."

"No, that's really not necessary..." the young leader protested.

"I won't take *no* for an answer" the man rebuffed.

He then proceeded to walk down the line and hand each of the reluctant men a five-dollar bill.

"Thanks again and stay safe". He turned and walked away. I tracked him until he disappeared into the station's Market Street vestibule and was gone.

A tongue clicked on the bench. Someone fidgeted with the multicolored ribbon on his breast pocket. Another removed imaginary lint from the gold epaulettes on his shoulder.

"Well", said the youngest looking of the group. "I suppose a free meal is a free meal. Who's for McDonald's?"

I was hungry myself, so I rose and fell in line behind them.

Me and four Delta Airline pilots.

William H. Graham III

A Beautiful Bike

My life changed ten years ago when my 19-year-old daughter suffered a brain injury. I had the choice to work and place her in a residential facility, or quit working.

I quit work and started living from government benefits. We have what's called NDIS (National Disability Insurance Scheme) here in Australia but it's a terrible system for people with special needs. It seems like our requests are always greeted with "No... No... No", and even when not turned down, there's always a lot of red tape to cut through.

One of my goals was to pick up an adult, three-wheeler bike for my child, and my application to the government was taking far too long. I scrimped and saved and found a Do-It-Yourself build kit on eBay for 500 Australian dollars, which was a major bargain. It took me over a week, and I watched a heap of Google videos in the process of building it, but I achieved it, and consider this my mightiest feat ever.

Not only was I so proud of this accomplishment, but my daughter loved it. I'd ride my electric scooter and she'd ride her bike with her trusty pup, *Fat Amy*, in the back basket. It was our joy. Some normalcy: the wind in our hair and smiles on our faces.

However, life changed dramatically again this year in February when the floods came to Queensland, Australia. We lost it all, apart from three bags of clothing. It was devastating. Everything I owned was gone. Even my daughter's beloved bike. I didn't know what to do, but badly wanted that feeling of bringing part of the world back for her so much. I needed that bike back!

Our lives have been so different from others, and things that make her life better do not fall in the usual priority list for others. But they really are priorities for her and for us.

I put out a call for a three-wheeler bike at a bargain price, as that bike had become so important to her. My call was answered, and more. We received one, kindly donated to us by two lovely people. She has a bike again, and it's made my heart so happy to see her rediscover her sense of joy.

These bikes are not cheap, and kindness counts so much. We are so grateful and overwhelmed by the kindness we have received. It's a beautiful thing from beautiful hearts. The best thing was seeing my daughter's face when we received this gift. She had lost everything: make-up, perfume, jewelry, her computer and her home gym were all gone. But her smile, through her tears of happiness, returned.

We ride together regularly now. The floods devastated our lives, but the kindness of others helped, and are helping rebuild it. We still are flood-affected and homeless but with the kindness shown, it's given me both hope and tears. Tears of gratefulness.

Thank you, kind-hearted people! You truly make a difference.

Julia Field-Mitchell

Black Bread and Herring

In the summer of 1990, the summer I turned 40, the summer the Berlin Wall fell, I traveled alone in Europe for several months, freely without visas.

I boarded a train in Poprad, northeastern Slovakia to go to Budapest then on to Greece. Around 7 in the evening, at the border with Hungary, the border patrol came to check passports.

An official who spoke passable English told me I could not enter Hungary without a visa. He ordered me to go back by train to Kosice, the last city in Slovakia we passed through, take a bus to the auto border crossing where I could get a visa, then take the bus back to the train station to get a train to Budapest. I tried everything to stay on the train—tears, anguish, bribery—but I was summarily booted off the train in the middle of nowhere in the dark. I must have looked a strange sight: a greying, solo American woman backpacker. Before I took the train back to Kosice, I asked the border official to write the instructions in my notebook so I could show it to someone for help. I could not speak or understand German or Czech or Hungarian.

At the bus station, I showed my notebook page to one driver after another. *No,* they waved, *not this bus, get off.* I showed a few people at the station my notebook page but was shooed away. I stared at the bus schedule sign, found no one at the ticket counter, and I realized there would be no bus or train tonight. It was after 10 p.m. by now and I was starting to lose it—my throat tightening, the tears starting. I was in trouble: this was an industrial concrete city with no tourist facilities, no hotels and no place for a taxi to take me. I needed safety, warmth and a place to pee. I walked in one direction, turned around, walked back and finally stood still staring at the schedule board with growing panic.

Suddenly there was a little voice at my shoulder.

"Chan I chelp you?"

I turned around to face a woman about my height and age, and answered *Yes, Please!* and crumbled into tears.

Her English was rough. She said the border official's instructions were right, but there were no buses going there tonight.

"You come home with me. I take you to bus in morning when I go to work."

Her name was Esther, a nurse at the local hospital coming off her shift. We took a local bus away from the city, down dirt side roads to her house. Esther insisted on paying the fare and practiced her English the whole ride. We entered a dark hall with pairs of shoes by the door, quietly, to not wake her mother and sister.

Her mother appeared moments later, a stout, elderly woman with grey hair pulled into a tight bun, a cotton apron housedress, her arms crossed over her wide breasts. Esther took me to the kitchen where I sat down at the table, exhausted from stress and a heavy pack, hungrier than I realized.

Esther's mother did not speak to me, did not smile, just stared at me with a stern expression, and asked Esther questions. Esther translated my responses, explaining the situation. Her mother's demeanor seemed disapproving. Esther busily moved about the kitchen, getting food for supper, practicing her English. I ate some herring, black bread, smoked cheese and tea. Esther was single, lived with her mother and sister, and was an Evangelical student. She spoke German, Hungarian, Czech and some French. Her family was Hungarian, living in the same place they had lived for generations, when it became part of Czechoslovakia after WWII.

Esther gave me a towel and directed me to the bath. A mere two hours before, I had visions of a cold bus bench or concrete floor, and here I was soaking in an old clawfoot bathtub, well fed and safe as a bug. Esther said she would wake me early at 5 a.m., showed me the daybed in her study, and said goodnight.

There was a long white cotton night dress with a lace collar and hem laying on the daybed, which sat under the largest velvet painting of Jesus I had ever seen. On the table were bibles and treatises and notebooks. I looked up at Jesus's face, and I suddenly understood the true meaning of Christianity. I wondered what Esther and her mother were thinking, having taken in this traveler, and what they would think about me being Jewish, the shtetl where my grandmother came from a few hundred miles north in Eastern Poland. Maybe it was people like Esther who took in Jewish refugees and hid them from Hitler. For once, I felt comforted by the Christian images surrounding me.

Esther woke me early, and by the time I dressed, she had a full spread for breakfast laid out for me (which I could barely eat), coffee, and a few things packed for my lunch. Her mother sat silently during our preparations, still with her harsh, disapproving stare. She spoke to Esther, I assumed telling her to check my backpack for stolen items, or to not bring strangers in the house again. Instead, she said to tell me that if I decided not to go to Budapest, I could stay at the house for as long as I wanted. She got up and said goodbye as we rushed out the door, a surprised expression of thanks on my face.

Esther put me on the right bus, and we said our goodbyes. We hugged, traded addresses, and I asked her what I could send in return for her generosity. She asked only for English study books. A month later in Greece, I lost my notebook with all my addresses. I couldn't send her the books I promised. I was distraught, thinking she would assume I did not care about what she did for me. My only solace was believing that Esther was a true Christian who

did what she did without expecting anything but the grace of God.

Cathy Dreyfuss

Three Heroic Strangers

In July 2015, I was working in Manhattan. I was meeting a client in Midtown East around 53rd Street. As I left the client and started walking towards the subway for my ride home, a giant thundercloud came over Manhattan. Lacking an umbrella and fully dressed in suit and tie, I decided to sprint the three blocks to the subway entrance.

However, in the last block, the skies opened up and rain poured down at a monsoon level. By the time I reached the top of the stairs to the subway, there was standing water on it. My feet shot out from underneath me, and I started falling down three flights of stairs. Without thinking, I saw a handrail and reached out with my right arm to grab it to stop my flight down the stairs—huge mistake!

All 203 pounds of me was flying downward at top speed. One arm reaching out and grabbing a stationary, solid object and… I completely dislocated my shoulder and still continued to tumble down the stairs to the bottom.

When I hit the bottom, my laptop and bag flew ten to fifteen feet from me, and my eyeglasses flew off. I even lost my wallet as I had it out to get to my Metro card. Lying on the ground, I could not even stand up to retrieve my stuff.

Out of nowhere, three people stopped and ran over to help. One person collected all my belongings and brought them to me. Another man ran up the stairs to call 911 and wait for the ambulance to direct them to where I was lying. A woman came and held my hand to comfort me until the paramedics arrived. We were still in the rain, she had no umbrella, yet she chose to stay there and get soaked to help me!

When the ambulance arrived, the second gentleman guided them down to me and took me to the hospital. He also called my family from my phone to let them know.

It was an incredible collective act of kindness by three strangers in a subway stairwell!

John T. Childress

Merit Badges

I grew up in a military family. We moved regularly, so I was always the new kid. And I had a hard time making friends. The toughest years for me were between fourth and sixth grades, when we were stationed in a small town in Germany.

I stood a foot taller than the other students. My clothes never fit right. Long sleeves stopped just past my elbows, instead of making their way to my wrists. Pants stopped several inches short of my ankles, and pedal pushers weren't in style then. I felt awkward and uncomfortable in my own skin. And kids pick up on that sort of thing. They sense when you are vulnerable.

A school bully named Danny made it his mission in life to torment me daily. While we waited for the morning bell to ring, he would steal my bag lunches, unwrap the sandwiches and throw them in the dirt. Or stomp on my Oreos, leaving only crumbs in the package. In dodge ball, he went after me in particular. I went home those afternoons with bright red welts on my skin where he hit me with the ball. And of course, he called me names like The Jolly Green Giant or Lurch, after The Addams Family came on TV. I wasn't well liked by anyone, even my teachers. All I wanted to do was stay in my room and read.

At home, my younger sister suffered from what was then called hyperactivity, now known as ADHD. She couldn't stop moving. At dinner, you just knew something was going to be spilled. My father took her behavior personally, as if she intentionally defied him. He wanted order in the house, and she was unable to comply. Every day felt like a war zone with him screaming at her, or slapping her upside the head. This meant Mom had to work overtime with my sister, to try and compensate for the damage Dad inflicted. Since I was quiet and uncomplaining, no one worried about me. I just gritted my teeth at his diatribes, and hid behind my books and colored pencils.

At some point, my parents decided I should join the Girl Scouts. I tried to get out of it. I knew it would just be another group of kids to make fun of me. But my parents insisted. I crept into the Scout room quietly and did my best to blend into the scenery.

Our troop leader, Mrs. Peterson, had two young children of her own. Unlike my teachers, she didn't allow me to sit silently in the back of the room. Rather, she encouraged me to actively participate with the group. "What do you think, Linda?" "Oh, that's a good idea. Why don't we try that?" She asked me for my opinions, and praised me when she thought I did something right. She provided all the attention I didn't get at home. And it worked. It turned out I was pretty good at those projects.

After a year, I was made a Patrol Leader, in charge of five other scouts. It's supposed to be an elected position, but my memory is that Mrs. Peterson just appointed me. I'm not sure. By that time, I was getting along with the other girls so it's possible they voted me in. It certainly surprised me enormously, but I took to the position well. When the troop met, we would split up into our patrols. I led my group in discussing which badges we would work on and how to best go about accomplishing our missions. It was a lot of fun, and I was proud and supremely surprised by my achievements.

Shortly before we left Germany, when I was twelve, the base had some sort of ceremony—perhaps it was for Memorial Day—and the Girl and Boy Scouts were invited to participate. Mrs. Peterson selected me to be the Girl Scout who would take the flag down. I was beyond shocked, and more than a little nervous. The ceremony would include not only the scouts but our parents and all the kids we went to school with.

It was rainy that day, so my mother insisted I wear her old raincoat. None of the other scouts wore one. And the Boy Scout who was assigned to walk with me was two years older and a head shorter than me. We were a comical sight, and Danny sneered at me when we passed our schoolmates. But it went off without a hitch and despite being embarrassed by my appearance, I felt enormously proud.

Mrs. Peterson's kindness made such a difference in my life. It gave me a confidence I had never had before. Even after we moved on to yet another Air Force base, I carried the lessons she taught me. I've never forgotten her, and have tried to pass on her good will to others. Paying it forward is the best way to honor her spirit.

Linda Shaffer

A Ring of Kindness

W hat were the odds?

The odds were stacked against me, so it helped that I wasn't really trying to succeed. Let me explain, while providing just a little background.

I've never been a big jewelry guy—to put it mildly. Other than a couple of inexpensive watches over the years— perhaps five years' worth—the only jewelry I've ever worn is my wedding band. In the 20 years I've been married, I've only taken my wedding band off to play sports or as required for certain medical procedures.

In the previous eight months, as a result of losing some weight and washing my hands thoroughly a zillion times a day, my ring had rolled off my finger several times but usually it had done so in my bathroom where I could either hear or see it. Except for a couple weeks prior to the following events when my faithful inanimate companion disappeared without a sound or a trace. Prior to this day, I had looked for it all around the house, to no avail.

That afternoon, the four of us—my wife, Ruby, son Benny and our tiny but sturdy Brussels Griffon, Knopa, and I—went for a nice walk around Columbia Lake, which is only about a mile from our home. As is our wont, it took us too long to get going, and we got started about one hour later than planned. On our otherwise enjoyable but unremarkable walk, I spotted a sign tacked to a tree. I had never seen a sign tacked to a tree surrounding Columbia Lake before.

The handwritten sign read, "RING FOUND", along with a phone number,

It couldn't be… could my ring have fallen off one day while taking a walk? It had previously only come off as a result of rigorous hand washing, or from my effortful tugging on my then-fattening finger before having x-rays performed.

Ruby agreed that it was worth a call, and as suspense goes, this isn't much of a story. A woman answered, and she seemed delighted that someone had called. As fate would have it, she picked up my call from the other side of the lake, where she and her husband were walking their dog. Columbia Lake is not exactly a major body of water: we probably could have conversed over soda cans and string.

After I described my ring, she seemed almost as relieved as I was. She explained that they had found the ring under some leaves a few days earlier, and yes, they had just posted the sign about 15 minutes before I saw it.

She asked if I would be kind enough to take the sign down and dispose of it, and then gave me their address. About 30 minutes later, I arrived to find her husband sitting in their front yard. He handed me an envelope and, with a little wink, asked me if I was sure that the ring inside was mine. I smiled and tried not to embarrass him by thanking him too profusely. They were simply nice, kind people. With the holidays approaching, I began to think of ways that I could somewhat repay their kindness.

The ring back on my finger—and yes, I tried to jam it on more snugly—Ruby suggested that we buy a lottery ticket. I thought about it for a moment or two. Let the record reflect that over the years, I've purchased almost as many lottery tickets as I have wedding rings. This was no small decision.

On the one hand (excuse the pun), why press my luck? But on the other hand, I figured the timing was as good as it would ever be for us.

What were the odds that the ring would ever be found, and *under* a pile of leaves?

What were the odds that the ring would be found by good, honest people who would take the initiative to post a sign?

I had no clue that the ring had come off at the lake. And what if we had walked around the lake in the reverse direction or had taken a walk elsewhere, for that matter?

What if we had left the house an hour earlier, as we had planned?

And what were the odds that we would be greeted with such nice, springlike weather? The next day, there was a deluge of cold, November rain.

I told Ruby that if we were ever going to hit the lottery, this would be the day.

Now, I'd love to be able to tell you that we hit the jackpot—even a small one—but I must let the truth get in the way of an even better story. No, we didn't. But we were already the recipients of great luck, impeccable timing and the kindness of someone from our own town.

Who could ask for more?

Matthew J. Goldberg

ACT Two

◊ ◊ ◊

"Kindness is more important than wisdom, and the recognition of this is the beginning of wisdom."

Aesop

Just A Dad

The year is 2005.

Every Wednesday at 2:00 p.m., I would bring Adam, my then-six-year-old son, to his aquatic therapy at Waterworks Aquatic Center in Irvine. I wheeled Adam into the building to the pool in his green Zippie-by-Quickie wheelchair with the cool metallic spokes. The pool was occupied by a handful of kids.

Poolside were all the moms. Only moms, sitting in the blue chairs around the water watching. Except for one very tall, younger looking man.

I noticed him a few weeks in a row, standing far away by himself at the other end of the pool. Then one day he approached me. He said, "May I ask you—what is wrong with your son?"

I don't usually like when people ask me that question, but he seemed genuinely concerned. He then said, "I am sorry. Did something happen to him? Why is he in a wheelchair? Can he walk? Do you mind if I sit next to you and watch him?"

"Sure," I said. We then began engaging in conversation. He was super curious.

"Would you mind if I talk to him after his lesson?"

I didn't mind, so I got Adam out of the pool, as the man got his daughter. Both of us parents wrapped our kids in towels. His daughter was a tiny toddler in a swim diaper, having actual swim lessons. I put Adam in his wheelchair. Then this lovely young man knelt down to him and said, "Hi. I'm Natalia's dad. Can I push you out to your car?" I thought it was a little strange that this dad took such interest in my kid, but my mom instinct told me that he was a good guy.

We all walked outside towards the van. A couple of younger teens approached the dad and asked for his autograph. They shouted, "Kobe! Kobe!" He was not thrilled to stop pushing Adam, but he did pause, signed something for them, and kept walking.

When we got to my van he said, "Adam, do you like basketball?"

Adam hadn't really seen basketball, so I was curious what his answer was going to be. He said *yes*, so Kobe said, "Maybe I could play basketball with you one day." As I held his daughter's hand, he lifted Adam into the car. I introduced myself and apologized that I hadn't recognized him.

"So sorry, Mr. Bryant. I thought you were just a dad."

He laughed and thanked me. "When I'm here, I *am* just a dad. Will you guys be here next week?"

"Yes, we come every Wednesday."

"Great. Adam, I will see you next week."

From then on, every Wednesday, Kobe brought Natalia into her swim lesson, then met us by the van. He would take Adam's wheelchair, then lift Adam out of his car seat for me and place him in his wheelchair. Adam has cerebral palsy, and his legs were so tight and tangled up, like a twisted pretzel. The two became good pals. After swimming, Kobe would chill with Adam for a while and show him some basketball dribbling moves.

This famous basketball star/father took time from his life to just spend time with my son, a kid with a disability. Not because of Make-A-Wish Foundation, and not because someone knew someone and made a phone call. No.

Because he was just a dad.

Ali Wolf

Kindness in the Time of Covid

I t's March, 2022. I've just come home from a rough day at work. If I'm honest, most of them have been rough days lately. This is a consequence both of my ambition (I've recently left a job I loved, to pursue a better opportunity) and my incompetence (I have not yet learned my new role well enough to be confident in the job I am performing). So, I would agree with anyone who said I had no one to blame but myself, but no one is saying that, at least not in so many words.

My wife is stressed. She also has a demanding career, one that she has to pour her heart and soul into, one that seeps into every aspect of her life and sometimes it seems like it takes her prisoner, locking her in a tower where she is bound by the relentless constraints of outcomes and expectations. Like me, she is incapable of accepting anything but her best, and it's becoming harder and harder

to excel in a world that seems to demand more and more from us all.

My son is at that awkward age where he is still testing limits. He's too independent to hold our hands in public anymore, but he looks for every opportunity to slide into our bed in the morning. We recently caught him in a lie, and not a little white lie, but a "look-me-in-the-eyes-and-swear" kind of lie. My wife was crushed, but I could at least see it for what it really was: another one of many developmental steps we all take on the journey from innocence to experience.

In an effort to let the stress of the day go, I sit down in a chair in the living room and listen to my wife talk about her day. As she does so, I'm making a mental note. Is she angry and looking to vent, or sad and looking for empathy? Occasionally it's both, and even though I am almost always quick to make suggestions, she is almost never looking for solutions, just someone to listen. Ironically, I realize I'm not actively listening to her at the moment, and I snap back into focus so I can absorb enough of the conversation to piece the rest together.

She senses that I'm not listening particularly well but what choice does she have? All our friends have their own lives with their own hurdles and their own struggles, and it's not as easy as meeting for coffee anymore. Every day we balance the risk of exposing someone we love to a virus that might make them sick with the risks of prolonged isolation, a risk we don't yet completely understand. But most of all, since we've been together for more than twenty years, we understand each other. That kind of history affords me the luxury of occasionally listening just enough to pass, but no more than occasionally.

The biggest difference between my wife and me is how we value certain things, people, places and experiences. I'm a history buff and a sucker for a good story. I collect baseball cards, old movies and, most recently, vinyl records. My wife collects books, at least to the extent that she buys them, reads them and sets them on a shelf where they are only subsequently moved when they've accumulated enough dust that a visible streak can be left by the trail of an inspecting finger. Most often she trades books among friends and has taken to listening to audio books to fill the brief spaces of time when she can't sit idly long enough to thumb through the pages. So, it could quite accurately be said that she doesn't collect anything and that her accumulation of books is more like the consequence of a reading addiction she can't ever seem to kick.

I have my own addictions, of course, and a basement full of boxes of baseball cards dating back through the decades allows me to trace the history of the great game by flipping through old carboard, looking at the uniforms and logos and how they've evolved, and wondering what life must have been like for a fifth-round draft pick from Topeka in the 1960s. The overwhelming majority of my collection has no monetary value, and I came to terms with that so long ago that pricing it out feels like a foreign concept. How can you put a price tag on memories?

Inevitably, however, everything comes at a cost, and my regular purchases of sports cards and memorabilia have added up to more than I'd like to admit. In an attempt to curtail my wife's consternation, I've evolved my thinking on making purchases for my hobby. I've narrowed my focus, choosing only to pursue the most elusive items and avoid the high-end items, and in doing so I've developed the self-restraint to avoid purchasing duplicates of anything I already have, regardless of how good a deal it seems to be.

It became clear, as the result of this change of course, that investing in the hobby was rarely providing me the kind of excitement and pleasure that it once had. To borrow a trending phrase, it no longer sparked joy, but I pushed that thought to the back of my head for the time being. Instead, as I was sitting on a chair in my living room, I picked my phone out of my pocket and as I usually do, I opened it and started to search local marketplace listings.

I typically search for baseball cards on a half dozen different sites each day, returning from time to time when I get the feeling something is out there waiting for me to discover. On this day, I was determined not to spend money on baseball items and thought I had outsmarted myself by searching for something else I liked to collect. At first, I searched for "Vinyl Records", and it's not like there aren't hundreds out there to choose from. I'm not much for classic rock and roll, however, and I never seem to see the kind I really like—Sam Cooke, Stevie Wonder or Marvin Gaye— wherever I look.

So, I searched again for something far less likely to have any results, but I was almost desperate. I thought of the old Warner Brothers movies and how I was starting to build a fine collection of hits like *The Maltese Falcon*, *The Treasure of the Sierra Madre*, and my personal favorite, *Casablanca*. Something about the classics awakens something in me. Maybe it's the tough-guy archetypes or the old-fashioned values, or the timelessness of stories about busting criminals and getting the girl. It's clear that part of me longs for a world that I never directly experienced, but through the magic of the motion picture, that world comes alive.

"Humphrey Bogart", I typed in the search bar, expecting to see no relevant results.

What I found instead was a curious chalkware art piece, too small to be a statue but too large to be an action figure, of Bogey in familiar *Casablanca* regalia—a tan overcoat and a numb expression like the woman he loved had just stood him up on a train platform in the pouring rain. Not only that, but next to it was a DVD of a Bogart and Bacall movie I hadn't seen—*To Have and Have Not*. My eyes beamed. This was the find of the year and it was reasonably priced, and when I checked the location, it was just a couple hours away, in my hometown.

Like most people, I've learned, I have a complicated relationship with my hometown. I would be inclined to call it love-hate, but I feel like that gives it entirely too much credit. In truth I was happy to leave and establish the life I have in the community I found, and I've done a thorough job of leaving my own past right where I left it.

I still had connections to my hometown, however, and I knew I could count on my dad to pick them up for me. I messaged the seller, offering to pick them up any time, and I awaited a response. When it came, they clarified that they were selling on behalf of someone else, and to make sure they were still available I should call a number provided and ask for a familiar name: Cecilia Burns.

Cecilia Burns. I stared at my phone in disbelief. I haven't lived in my hometown for twenty years. The number of people who live there that I might still remember, or that might remember me, must be practically infinitesimal. What were the chances that the person selling these items would be my old second grade teacher, the kind lady who was so gentle and caring and who, in my second-grade report card called me a "very mature student", and one she was very proud of? At the end of the year, to show her gratitude for my efforts through the year, she gave me an enormous hardcover book on dinosaurs that I flipped through dozens of times over the subsequent years.

It was an overwhelming moment in which I realized I had repressed so much of my own youth, and all the anger and frustration of my teenage years that I had poured over every memory was suddenly wiped away... if not entirely, then perhaps enough for me to see a clear picture through on the other side. Suddenly I'm sitting in my second-grade class again, at an elementary school that has long been closed, listening to her read stories and reassure me when I got an answer wrong on a test. I hated being bad at anything back then, and I see so much of myself in my son who stubbornly refuses to accept that there is so often a learning curve with most things worth doing.

But what made Cecilia Burns special was the way she made you feel when you were her student. She embraced you, often literally, as if you were her own child. She made sure we felt valued and heard, and she went above and beyond to express how important we all were. The enormity of buying a book for me out of her own pocket only sunk in when I became an adult, and it suddenly meant even more to me long after I got over my fleeting fascination with Tyrannosaurus Rex.

I wondered if I was going to be able to make the call. I was nervous, holding the phone in my hand, wondering if I should even mention that I was once her student. Frankly, it was thirty-five years ago, and she had a long teaching career. Part of me wondered if she would remember me and another part understood how foolish an expectation that would have been.

I decided, with some trepidation, to call, and when the voice answered on the other end it was a man's voice. Once I explained the purpose for my call I was asked to hold for the "Humphrey Bogart lady", and I waited. A few seconds later, a soft voice came on the phone and said hello. For about a minute or so we spoke. I asked about the statuette and the DVD and she said that yes, they were still available. I told her my dad would pick them up and we chatted briefly about classic movies. She said she struggled with technology, but she always watched classic movies when she was lucky enough to find one on cable. She had the items listed for long enough that she doubted that anyone still liked Humphrey Bogart.

I told her about my love for classic movies and how Bogart was one of the best actors of his generation. In fact, I was building something of a collection now, and these would fit right in. We were both satisfied, and it appeared the conversation was approaching a natural conclusion when I decided to use the opportunity to speak up.

"Did I understand correctly that I'm speaking to Cecilia Burns?" I asked.

"Yes," she answered, "this is Cecilia Burns."

I don't know the precise physiology of what happened but when she confirmed that, I was overwhelmed by a sudden warmth that folded over me like I had been dipped in warm honey.

"Well, Mrs. Burns, I happen to be one of your former students at Arcadia School," I said, beaming. I told her my name, told her where I lived now and how my father still lived in Arcadia. I also told her how I distinctly remember how warm and kind she was, and how great it was to be her student.

She was surprised, I'm certain, though I do suppose this isn't the first time she's been contacted by a former student. No one teaches for decades without generating a massive, lasting network of influence.

She told me she loved teaching, that fond memories of those years still fill her with joy, and she thanked me effusively for my call. I told her about the dinosaur book, and thanked her again, more than three decades after the first time, for her generosity.

What struck me the most was her self-awareness. She admitted, candidly, that the kindness she demonstrated was a deliberate effort, that there were enough strict and imposing authorities in our children's lives that someone needs to be a comfort. Someone needed to be a support, a safe place, and a person they can count on for compassion and acceptance. Indeed, the world is full of difficult people and even more difficult situations, and she aimed to represent a reprieve, if ever so briefly, in the hearts of youths.

I thanked her for her impact on me and how she shaped my view of the world. I was a tender-hearted young man, subsequently served a series of rough lessons on my way to adulthood, but I deferred always, or at least as much as I could, to treating others with respect. The world is so often such a cruel place that to reach adulthood with any semblance of care for others feels like a victory, and though I no longer wear my heart on my sleeve as outwardly as I once did, I understand that I was shaped by the early example of a thoroughly caring and wonderful teacher.

When we hung up the phone, I was overwhelmed by a sense of guilt that I hadn't said precisely the right thing or hit the right tone. It had been so long since my last opportunity and I might not get another, so I regretted not speaking longer or not having something more impactful to say. My fears were eased when my dad called later that night to explain he had visited Cecilia Burns to purchase the items, and she refused.

She told him she would not accept any money for the items, that she was happy to give them to someone who would appreciate them, and she was so very grateful for our conversation. I told him I wasn't surprised whatsoever, that another act of kindness was completely in character, and there was something so wonderful about accepting that in this crazy world, some things really do never change.

In the weeks since my conversation with Cecilia Burns, I've forced myself to reevaluate my priorities. I've become a more disciplined and careful listener. I've spent more time with my son, and I've caught up with friends I hadn't seen in too long. I'm understanding the great lesson in all this, the value of people and places over things, and the power and wisdom of forgiveness. More and more it has become obvious to me that it is our shared responsibility to spread kindness in the world, that kindness itself remains highly contagious and there is no cure or a vaccine.

I have no false expectations that I will have the kind of lasting influence of Cecilia Burns, but it's a lofty goal, and I am a better person for aiming at that kind of legacy.

Matt Clairmont

The 100-Dollar-Bill Story

"Money on its own means nothing. A one-hundred-dollar bill sitting on a table is a piece of paper. It's the energy around it that makes it relevant. That one one-hundred-dollar bill could have been slipped into a birthday card by your granny, or you could have stolen it from your best friend when she wasn't looking, or you could have earned it by doing something that you loved, or you hated."

This is an excerpt from the Jen Sincero book, *You Are a Badass*. I was reading it on a long car trip with my family.

My husband, our six-month-old son and I were on a seven-hour car ride from Pensacola to Tampa, Florida. We were snuggly packed into our blue Honda Civic. Eventually, we had to pull off the highway to get something to eat. My husband wanted a very particular local fast-food fried-chicken restaurant. Going to this place was adding a good 20–25 minutes to our drive. "It better be good," I said.

The book was in the self-help category. For the longest time, I couldn't get myself to pick it up. The title seemed to scream, *You need help!* Nonetheless, it had a profound effect on me. Just as we were pulling up to this gotta-have-fried-chicken joint, I finished reading the page in the book that asked its readers to do an exercise: "Sit your broke ass down and write a letter to money…"

I thought: *This is cute, but I don't have any issue with money.* At the time, I was working a nine-to-five, driving a Honda, and never questioned my lifestyle. I closed the book and went on with my life. It was finally time to stretch our legs.

We made our way inside, and I was utterly unimpressed. I picked a table and started giving my son a bottle while my husband ordered. The place was empty, except for a group of four—two older couples—sitting in the back of the restaurant. Our food was ready just as they were walking out.

Suddenly, one of the women started to sway and stumbled into one of the tables. I couldn't help but stare, as something about this scene was really odd. The woman recovered, took a couple more steps, and started sliding onto another table. Without taking my eyes off her, I shoved my son into my husband's arms. He was confused. I said: "Take him…now!"

I ran up to the woman as she was still fighting gravity. Her body was sprawling across the table, dripping over onto the neighboring booth seat. My heart was pounding, as I thought she was having a heart attack.

I lowered her onto the seat and got on my knees, trying to look her in the face for any other signs of a medical emergency. Was she perfusing? Was she having difficulty breathing? Was she pale? I took her hands and kept asking: "What is it? Are you ok?" She finally looked up at me with embarrassment and said:

"I have MS."

"Oh, just MS? Thank God! I thought you were having a heart attack!"

My reply came out selfishly. We both let out a laugh and it felt like a gasket was released. She said: "Many people think I am drunk in the middle of the day, it's really embarrassing."

MS stands for multiple sclerosis. It is a disease wherein the body attacks the sheath that covers the nerves. Because the sheath can no longer conduct the signal, the motor function of the body gets severely impaired. For her, an attack happened as they were walking out. She was in her late 50s or early 60s, and she was recently diagnosed, but the progression of her disease was fast. She never knew when these episodes would come on, so they often happened in public. She recalled how one woman publicly scolded her, telling her she should be ashamed of herself because that other woman thought she was intoxicated.

For four years, I worked as a Doctor of Physical Therapy at one of the country's top neurological rehab facilities. I loved gait training people who were recovering from spinal cord injuries and brain injuries. During that time, I also had a few patients who had MS.

We both knew that even though she wasn't having a heart attack, that MS will one day leave her bedridden, and that day was coming soon. We laughed some more; we cried some more. Completely outside of my usual restrained self, I told her: "I love you." I helped her walk to her car. Slowly we got into their truck. She mustered every ounce of will and strength to walk the short distance. I was proud of the fight in her.

There was an undeniable dynamic of reciprocal acts that led to an instant connection. She was willing to accept help and therefore allow me to feel good. And her husband couldn't thank me enough.

He said he felt terrible that he couldn't physically help her. He was recovering from recent heart surgery, and he wasn't supposed to lift more than 10 pounds. Just as I was about to head back inside, the husband stretched out his hand to me. He was holding a 100-dollar bill. I froze for a second, thinking, *Should I take it?*

I said: "No, no, no! I can't possibly take it. That's not why I did it. It would make this whole thing seem wrong." Before my crude decline, there had been so much love and connection between us perfect strangers, but I then could feel the energy shift. The wife looked embarrassed, and the man looked dumbfounded. Their friends who were standing in a circle did not know what to say. It was an awkward moment for everyone present.

The man tried to play it off: "Oh, it's just a dinner, on us." But I continued to push my selfless hero act. Finally, the friend intervened and said: "Just let it be. You are embarrassing her." We said some more goodbyes, and I went back inside.

The whole event left me riding an adrenaline wave, but it wasn't over. As soon as we got back in the car, I started nearly screaming at my husband. I was trying to tell him about what had just happened. It came out something like this.

"Babe! I was just reading this book! And they have an exercise about a 100-dollar bill! And you're supposed to write down what you think about it! And I thought it was stupid! But this man just offered me a 100-dollar bill, and I turned it down. But now I want it! OMG, I think money is dirty!"

My husband was merging on the highway and shifting gears as I was trying to get this out. Our precious 2008 Honda Civic didn't have much power. We quickly got passed by a white pickup truck. His license plate said: HVEFATH, or *HAVE FAITH*. I was beside myself, completely exuberant. I said: "Babe, Babe, look at that truck's license plate!!!" Even my fully rational and logical husband couldn't help but smile.

Looking back on it, I was the perfect person to help that woman at that moment. And that family and that book were the perfect teachers for me.

But besides the lesson on money, I could no longer deny that a supreme power exists. Something beyond us that's always there, regardless of our level of awareness. It gave me chills. I ordered the same custom plate as I saw on that truck. I hope it gives someone else a much-needed message when the time is right. It is a simple reminder to have faith in life's detours, have faith in yourself, and have faith in the magnificent universal soul that connects us all.

Svetlana Mellein

A Faint Memory

The door pinged and closed behind me, and I held onto a metal pole for support. The train started to rumble, and we were off. But suddenly, I was also off.

It was a New York day of being in my 20s and running around the city, and I was ready to get home. The air was humid and sticky, and I felt brief relief in the air-conditioned subway car. I had dashed through the New York underground on my way to the train, at pace with the human traffic, chin up. But now there was a rhythm to the car on the track that made me sleepy, and I felt my skin feel cold and sweaty all at once.

I tried to focus on standing, but my knees seemed to keep buckling under me. There was a man standing next to me in a suit, and I just remember the tie and the jacket, but no face. It was like I couldn't lift my head high enough to see him.

I wondered if people recognized something was wrong, or if they thought I was on drugs. I had dressed nicely that day, for reasons I don't recall: a form fitting blue vest, jeans, my hair clipped back, artsy jewelry I had pulled out of cobwebs. Surely, I looked sensible enough, I thought, but my cognition started to fade.

The train stopped. The muffled subway announcer said, "Last stop before Brooklyn." I heard the doors ping behind me, and a woman shot up from her seat across from me.

"Are you okay?" she asked.

"I think I'm fainting," I replied, my eyes at half-mast.

She proceeded to push me out the door. "You need to get off the train," she said. The blood, however, was not reaching my brain and I just flopped around like a standing noodle. My arm blocked the door, and it bounced open again. Ping. It tried to close. "You need to get off the train," she said again.

And finally, with the next door opening, she successfully hoisted us both out onto the platform.

I melted into the crack against the wall, and sat on the stained cement. The train shuffled away down a dark corridor to what seemed like a final, dark portal, and we sat on the brightly-lit edge of infinity. The woman sat next to me. We were alone.

"I don't think I ate enough today," I managed to eke out.

She took some chocolates from her bag and a plastic water bottle. "Drink this slowly," she instructed. "And nibble on the chocolate." She watched attentively as I obeyed.

Slowly, my mental faculties returned, and what had been a watercolor world refocused into a modern painting. The woman had brown hair, and couldn't have been more than thirty. She was on the petite side, like me. I began to get chatty and felt a wave of embarrassment come over me.

"I don't know what happened, thank you so much. I've never fainted before. I guess I didn't eat enough," I stammered on.

"Just take your time," she said. She explained that she worked in a medical setting and always carried water and chocolates just in case, and she, herself, was a fainter.

We let one train pass, then eventually got on the next one. I felt perfectly fine and totally mortified. I repeated it to her enough times that despite her seemingly shy disposition, she confessed that this was not the least bit embarrassing compared to her own fainting stories. "Oh?" I asked.

"Well, I was holding up a canopy at my friend's wedding. There were four of us, each holding a corner. My husband and I and two other friends. And it got long, and I guess I locked my knees, and I just fainted on the spot and dropped the canopy on the bride and groom, and my husband, of course, came running to help me and dropped his as well."

I laughed in relief at her story, and the comedic imagery of it, though I could see it was very painful for her to recount. She felt she had ruined her friend's wedding.

"That is very mortifying," I said. "Thank you for sharing to make me feel better about this."

Eventually, she saw that I was okay, and she exited at her stop in Brooklyn, and I carried on a little longer. I don't remember her name. I don't remember her face. I later imagined the horror of fainting in the subway car and the mayhem that would have ensued had she not helped me. Not to mention any injuries I would have had from falling.

What were the chances that a woman who recognized fainting would be sitting across from me on the subway the day I almost fainted? She did not need to help me. She could have continued ignoring what was happening—like *Suit Guy*. She was my subway angel that day, and I am grateful for the small piece of human generosity that protected me in such a vulnerable moment.

Deanna Neil

Just in Time

I was around six or seven years old in St. Croix when Mommy and Daddy got me in the car and headed eastbound to someone's home on the north side of the island, a few miles shy of Cramer's Park Beach. I didn't know the people we were visiting, but as a bartender, Daddy met many adults who left the States to enjoy the all-year-round warm sun and turquoise Caribbean Sea waters.

After we arrived, I sampled the hors d'oeuvres while I tuned out the conversation between my parents, their acquaintances, and a neighbor who'd stopped by.

A few minutes later, a little blonde girl tapped my shoulder and asked, "You want to see something?"

"Sure," I said, longing for a break from the droning on of grown-up conversation.

I followed the girl away from the townhouse, walked across the small road my parents and I had traveled in on, and trotted down a long roadway toward a single home overlooking the sea surf washing onto the sand in the distance below.

The single-story house sported tinted windows all around with a sliding door on the other side.

I took tentative steps, concerned about the lack of adult supervision. I'd never wandered out of my parents' sight at an unfamiliar location before. "Are you sure it's okay I'm here?"

"Yes, it's fine. I know this house." The girl's smile calmed me a little, but the strange wiggly worms in my gut wouldn't dissipate.

I stayed a good twenty feet or so behind her as she tiptoed toward the sliding doors. I had my doubts that she should be doing what she was about to do. I glanced back up the sloping driveway, but no one approached.

A loud, aggressive bark made my abdomen drop and the hairs on my skin stand on end. The sight of a huge German shepherd bounding toward me activated my flight response. I turned and sprinted as fast as my skinny legs allowed.

Having grown up with mixed breed dogs, I was rather familiar with canine traits. This lunging ball of fur was not the friendly kind, at least not to me. It had brushed right past the little girl to chase the outsider—me. I was trespassing on its domain.

I don't remember screaming, but I must have. I called for Daddy, the one person I knew who could rescue me from this animal. I'd never met a dog who didn't like me. Why didn't this one?

I glanced back to find the dog gaining on me. I pushed ahead harder than I ever had in my short life. I thought I'd lived my last day. Figures of adults—tears blurred my eyes from deciphering how many—cleared the far corner, but I didn't think any of them would reach me in time. I could almost feel the hot breath and saliva of the now jaw-snapping hound.

Twisting a bit to view my assailant, any remaining hope had bolted. The German shepherd bounded two more times when hands surrounded my waist and lifted me out of reach of the snarling animal. At first, I figured Daddy had gotten to me in time, but the height difference where I'd rested my head on a shoulder alerted me that the person who held me was a stranger.

I peered up into the face of a white man, maybe the girl's father, but definitely the dog's owner because the German shepherd no longer saw me as a meal. It sat and panted as if nothing was amiss in the world.

Meanwhile, my heart pounded as I snuggled my head in the crook of this man's neck and cried.

Daddy reached us seconds later, and I extended my arms toward him. His distressed features relayed to me that he regretted not being fast enough. He turned to the man and thanked him for getting to me in time.

I vaguely remember some scolding of the girl going on as Mommy hugged me close. The little girl had been tiptoeing because she wasn't allowed to let the dog out of the house without her dad.

Even after all these years, I still remember the fright, but the rescue saved me from a marred body and enabled me to maintain my love for animals, including canines. I remain grateful that someone my parents had just met did all he could to get to me just in time.

Cassandra Ulrich

An Agreement is an Agreement

When your kid calls you and starts out the conversation with, "Mom, Dad, I'm Okay", you know the rest of the story is going to give you retroactive parent stress. Our 25-year-old son called us to let us know that about a half an hour ago, he was driving and had knocked a side mirror off a parked car.

Our son pulled over and assessed the damage. The owner of the parked car was nowhere to be seen but the mirror was definitely detached from the car and laying underneath it. He then put the broken mirror next to the car and wrote the owner a note. He explained what happened, and gave the car owner my husband's name and phone number.

Then he called his dad, who immediately put him on speaker phone. After he told us what had happened, I said,

"Well of course, the important thing is that you are okay. By the way, what kind of car did you hit?"

His answer made both our blood pressures rise. "A Tesla", he said.

"A TESLA?? You hit a TESLA???" were the only words that came out of my mouth. Knowing the price of a Tesla, I could only imagine the mirror was going to cost thousands of dollars to replace.

A few hours later, his dad got a call from the owner of the Tesla who identified himself as Scott. He was very nice, and my husband told him we had a great place for him to take his car to assess the damage. He agreed to take it there.

Our son called us back a few minutes later, saying he'd forgotten to tell us that he had taken some pictures at the scene. He sent them to us, and we saw what he had seen: that the car was parked well beyond the *No Parking* arrows.

We regarded this as a brilliant move on his part. I then composed a text to Scott, letting him know that his Tesla was actually in a dangerous spot around a curve in the road. Perhaps, that is one of the reasons it got hit. I asked him if he would consider, maybe, splitting the cost, given the car was parked precariously.

Scott quickly responded. "I am just appreciative of the fact that your son left me a note. "Not everyone would do that." He immediately agreed to split the cost, half and half.

We were very relieved, and appreciated his response so much. We just knew that not everyone who had just gotten his beautiful, expensive car damaged would have responded that way.

A few days later, we got a message from Scott that the cost of the mirror repair was going to be $500. We were further relieved, thinking it was going to be so much more! As agreed, we immediately forwarded him the $250 and were happy for the amicable resolution. We thought that this was the end of the saga.

About three days later, to our surprise, we received a payment for $80. We wondered, *Who sent us $80 and for what?* I examined the payment, and realized it was from Scott. He had included the following note: "Hi, this is Scott, the owner of the Tesla. When I went to pick up my car following the repair, the bill turned out to be $160 less than they had quoted me. We spoke of a 50-50 agreement and because it was less than expected, I'm forwarding you your $80."

To this day, it is one of the kindest things anyone has done for us, and his gesture absolutely restored our faith in humanity. It underscored what we've always hoped for— that there really are kind, decent people that stick to their agreements.

Dee-Dee Sberlo

A Labor of Love

When I delivered my son, I experienced a rather traumatic labor. My epidural did not work, and after multiple rounds of the medication, the doctors finally redid the epidural. The extreme numbness of my body sent me into a panic attack.

As I neared delivery, the nurses and my husband tried to calm me down. I was still in extreme pain from how my son had positioned himself in my body. While one of the nurses told me, "That's labor," another nurse felt quite concerned for my health. She stayed by my side, talking to me and bringing me ice.

I had developed a fever, and she surmised it was from the epidural. She did not leave my side, but her shift ended at 7 p.m., just as I started the pushing phase of my delivery. My son made his entrance into this world at 8:56 p.m. on a Tuesday. Both my son and I had a relatively high fever when he was born, and they carted him off to the NICU (Newborn Intensive Care Unit) to make sure he didn't have sepsis. He would stay there for 48 hours before they determined whether or not he had it or could be returned to my husband and me. We were able to visit him as often as we liked, and, thankfully, he did not have sepsis.

On Wednesday and Thursday that week, my husband and I were in and out of the NICU visiting my son. On Thursday, I heard my Facebook messenger chime, and I checked it. This is the message I received.

"Hi Stefani, this is your nurse Stephanie, from the other day. I'm so sorry to reach out to you like this on Facebook, but I *had* to find out how you were doing. I was off on Wednesday, but as soon as I got to work on Thursday morning, I went to your room. When I saw you and your husband weren't there, I got worried. Is your son okay? Does this mean he was in the NICU? I was so worried about you, and I want to make sure you and your baby are both doing well. Again, I am so sorry to reach out like this."

I remember reading it and tears immediately filling my eyes. I don't have good experiences with the medical system. My mother spent her last days in a hospital where the nurses and doctors were uncaring and insensitive. To see this woman going out of her way to find me and ask about me when she certainly didn't have to, made me feel pure gratitude. Of course, I responded and told her the good news. I am so thankful to her for being there for me the day my son was born and for going out of her way to check up on me.

To this day we are Facebook friends, and I just learned that she earned a prestigious Nursing Excellence award, an honor that she certainly deserves.

Stefani Milan

Kindness is Coolness

Is there a kindness too big or too small? Every little act can set more acts in motion. How often do we see people thanking others for coffee or for a drive-through treat in a random Dunkin' line?

Sometimes, people create giant kindness waves. For me, small moments count just as much as these larger waves.

On New Year's Eve circa 2002, a friend and I were having a drink on the quiet side of a bar that had two different entrances. A stranger sitting next to us asked why us young gals weren't in the big party next door. We smiled, and said we just weren't up for it. Truthfully, the cover charge was about $60 apiece, and being fresh out of college, we couldn't afford it. After about an hour sitting and conversing, he handed us money for the cover and wished us *Happy New Year.* We've called him our New Year's Angel ever since.

My father passed away while I was in college. And when I summered down the shore, one of my new friends invited me to stay over after a night out. The next day when I went to leave, her parents asked me to stay. They told me that they would wash my work uniform with their kids' clothes, and that way, I could go to the beach and back to work without running around and stressing out. They didn't know me from anyone, but found the kindness in their hearts to continue to bestow these parental acts on me. I became a fourth child to them, and we've celebrated life events—both happy and sad—for more than 20 years now. To this day, I wish them *Happy Parent's Day*, and tear up at the thought of their generosity.

When I moved into my first New York City apartment, my boss at the time asked me what I needed. I told him that I had to supply my own air conditioning unit. He handed me a personal blank check, so I could purchase an air conditioner unit and have it delivered and installed. He wanted to ensure I would be more comfortable in my new home, with no discussion about money, work time or anything else. His act of generosity changed my month financially—and saved my day from having to carry the unit and learn how to install it.

Sometimes, it's the kindness we share with strangers or pets or animals that makes life special. When you help someone with no expectation of anything in return and without the plan to publicize it, you put good out in the universe and end up feeling so good, too. It's food for the soul. One small act of kindness can change the course of another person's life. It can turn a bad day good, change perspectives, and even inspire someone else.

In my opinion, kindness is coolness.

Lauren L. Sullivan

Fun and Games... and Finances

Sometimes, what seem like small gestures from the giver mean so much more to those who receive that gift. Here are two examples that I am fortunate to count among my life experiences.

One of my memories growing up in Manila, The Philippines is that of my dad buying us a ping pong table when I was in high school. Dad was an avid basketball and tennis player who also enjoyed ping pong. I still recall his funny trick of faking his shots by looking to the right then quickly placing the ball in the left corner. It was generally effective until I gradually started to catch on.

Our table was a hit with my two brothers and me, and with many others in my neighborhood. Friends and family frequently came over to play. One guest named Alex noticed my potential in the sport and started to offer lessons to me. I learned that he was a professional player when he was younger. This generous man gave me a book on how to play well and came to our place several times to give me free table tennis lessons.

Soon, I became quite adept, and won several competitions in our school. At one point, I even became the president of our table tennis club. I have learned to love the game and still have a lot of fun playing ping pong today. My mentor, Alex, never asked for anything in return. He shared his time and expertise willingly without any expectations.

Alex would not be my only kind mentor along the way. When I came to the U.S. at age 23, I didn't realize that there were so many nuances that I had to know about in order to thrive. At that young age, all I thought about was my new career as a physical therapist and enjoying my new environment of Queens, New York City. The notion of having good credit was never in my thoughts, nor was the idea of making investments and the yearning to own my own house.

Luckily for me, one doctor I was working with shared what I needed to do in order to start accruing good credit. A little later on, another doctor advised that I ask my landlord to sell to me the apartment I was living in. I would have never thought about taking such a huge step had he not encouraged me to do so.

These steps have helped me tremendously to be disciplined with my finances. These two angels did not have to teach me anything, since they were not even my friends or relatives. Each of them took the time to sit me down in their offices to make sure I understood how important it was to know how to survive in the U.S.

Even though both these instances happened more than 20 years ago, I still vividly remember them and am grateful for the kind advice they gave me at those important times in my life.

Anna Factor

Opportunities

With G-d's grace, I was never taught or encouraged how to hate another person due to their skin tone, religious beliefs, or lifestyle choices. Live and let live! Racism, bigotry, and homophobia reside in fear, and it's easy, too easy, to live in hostility.

A few days after the 911 attacks, I found myself in line waiting to order coffee and grab a bagel. The usual chatter and smiles morphed into an eerie silence as we grieved noiselessly. A gentleman took his place online and stood quietly, avoiding eye contact. He could feel our collective icy stares and discomfort for no reason other than the burgundy turban wrapped on his head. I was not proud of my feelings of contempt, bitterness, and disfavor that sunny morning in Mount Kisco, New York. But they were there.

Fast forward a few months. I'm one of those drivers who gets lost as soon as I cross the New Jersey border. As I left my weekend job in Paramus, I was tired, hungry, and eager to get back to Westchester. It didn't take long for me to make a series of wrong turns and find myself entirely lost.

I stopped at a gas station and asked a teenager for directions but received a complete set of misdirection. I always thought that was intentional and began humming George Harrison's *Blue Jay Way* as I drove aimlessly. "We'll be over soon, they said, now they've lost themselves instead."

The further I drove out of my way, the more anxious I became. I pulled over to compose myself when a Chevy Blazer pulled in behind me. A tall gentleman wearing a dark turban walked over to my car and asked if I was alright. He recognized my anxiety and asked how he could help. Within minutes, he offered to lead me back to the Garden State Parkway, and my world became sane again.

Years later, I was driving to an appointment and noticed a grey sedan pulled over with the emergency lights blinking. This gentleman, who happened to be wearing a turban, was late for an interview and frustrated. I previously thought of my good fortune in Jersey and stopped to offer assistance.

There are no coincidences, just G-d's way of staying anonymous. He told me that I was the only one who had stopped and was grateful. I knew how he felt and invited him to follow me as I drove to his destination.

As the great baseball icon and humanitarian Roberto Clemente once said, "Any time you have an opportunity to make a difference in this world, and you don't, then you are wasting your time on Earth."

Scott Paul Goldman

You're Always Welcome Here

Having stood as the Mecca of freedom, America has been attracting people from all over the world who are seeking a new and better life for their families. The people who have been suppressed and deprived unquestionably cherish every single day living in the United States. I'm one of them.

I came to study here just for fun but later realized I had to bring my family over to the Mecca that upholds human rights. At least, the ideology has been executed way better than where I was born and raised.

Immigrating to the U.S. has been the furthest thing from easy for international students. I found no excuses, though, and always strived to prove myself worthy of becoming a U.S. permanent resident and eventually a citizen. It's been an adventure, but I had never questioned my determination until the pandemic happened.

One day in Marina del Ray, California, while I was waiting in line to check out my groceries, I heard these words from a man in his 50s:

"Where're you from?"

"Huh?"

"Where're you from?" He asked again.

"China, " I replied.

"What're you doing here?"

"What do you mean?"

"What're you doing here?"

I was a bit confused at first, but sort of saw what was coming. "Getting groceries?"

"Why did you bring this virus to my country? Go back to China."

I had been seeing so many similar incidents on the news but never thought this could happen to me one day. I am an adult, and I wanted to handle this myself instead of seeking help from law enforcement. I tried to remain calm. "I wish I could, but I can't go back to China. I need to stay here."

"No, we don't want you here. Look what you have done." He pinched his mask.

"I've been staying here in The States since August, 2019. It wasn't me. Plus, the last virus I got was ten years ago from my computer when I watched a movie."

I tried to use my humor to soften the situation. It didn't work for him. "All you Chinese people are just nasty. Y'all *effed* up the world. Go back where you belong."

"I'm here trying to seek a new life for the family, just like your ancestors. Also, it wasn't the Chinese people's fault but the failure of the government."

He had no interest in responding further, so he packed his groceries. He flipped me an obscene gesture, and left.

I was both furious and depressed. I was on the edge of screaming and cussing at him. *Why do these kinds of people exist?* I shook my head, suddenly losing hope in this country: this Mecca, the future second home where I've been working so hard to get my Green Card. I started to lose interest when all of a sudden, I heard: "Don't listen to him. He is an idiot."

I turned around, and saw a woman who looked to be in her 50s. "He doesn't represent us. You're always welcome here."

I nodded to her and squeezed out a smile. "Thank you."

"He doesn't represent us. You're always welcome here. He doesn't represent us. You're always welcome here. He doesn't represent us. You're always welcome here."

Her simple, kind and empathetic words were echoing in my head. After I checked out my groceries, I turned my head one more time. "Thank you again."

Those simple, kind words saved my American dream.

Boliang "Michael" Wang

ACT Three

◊ ◊ ◊

We can't solve all the mysteries
of the complex human mind
We can explore for months and years
not sure what we will find
So please be open-minded
and most of all be kind.

Matthew J. Goldberg

The Tiny Mayor

I am six years old and not terribly socialized. In fact, I'm kind of wild. Big curly hair, mischievous eyes, and a high-pitched laugh. In my father's words, I'm quite a rascal. Cute, but a rascal.

I live in a big, rambling Victorian house that is two houses slammed together. There's a wide-open seam in the house where the two structures meet and multiple places for me to vanish. It's amazing this house hasn't swallowed me up. I torment the house as much as it torments me. My mother torments me, too. She wasn't ready for motherhood.

Shortly after my birth, it became clear that my mother had been living with mental illness and had hidden it very well from my father. She sleeps, a lot. In fact, she sleeps so much I have the run of the house, the yard, and the neighborhood. I'm the tiny mayor of my street. Everyone knows me.

I wander into apartment buildings and have meals with people I've just met. My favorite new neighbor is Mr. Andrews, an elderly man living on the second floor of the heavily ivied apartment building next to my house. I walk into his apartment once a week. He sets up a TV tray, cooks up a Swanson's Hungry Man meal and we watch *Bewitched* together.

One day, after our lunch from inside Mr. Andrews's apartment, I hear my mother calling for me from our porch. Just randomly screaming my name out to the universe, hoping that some child that looks like me will appear.

Panicked, I run down to our front yard, under our huge rubber tree. I'm just out of sight.

"Sean, where the hell are you?!" my mother yells. My mother stands there in her pink fuzzy bathrobe she never takes off. Like a figurehead on the bow of a ship, she calmly waits for an answer.

"I'm out playing…" I reply.

I need to use the bathroom badly. The *Hungry Man* isn't sitting well. But I know if I go back in the house, my mother won't let me out again. I decide to pull down my pants and poop in the front yard, where everyone can see me, except my mother. I wipe my butt with a rubber tree leaf. It doesn't work very well. It's too smooth and doesn't get the job done. I give up, hike up my pants and take off down the street, ignoring my mother's voice.

As I run down the street, I see a young girl with brown hair, about my age, with her stylish grandmother on their front porch. I stop, hypnotized. It looks like a movie set. The house is beautiful, a huge colonial style structure with big white pillars. The lawn is immaculate, a stark contrast to my house. I've never seen this home before. How have I missed this? The tiny mayor knows all!

"Lisa," the grandmother coos, "be careful!"

"I'm fine," Lisa says.

Lisa stands up and she has a crutch under each arm. She drags herself down the immaculate lawn with her dolls and sets up shop. She manually picks up each of her legs and positions herself neatly. Her grandmother follows her with a tea set, then retreats to the porch.

Lisa catches my eye. "Hi," she says.

"Hi," I reply. "I'm the mayor of this street. That's what my dad calls me." Lisa looks up at me with a sad, warm smile. She looks tired.

Lisa says, "Wanna play?"

"Yes," I say.

I crawl up over the fence and on to the manicured lawn. I sit across from Lisa. Everything looks so nice. The dolls, the lawn, the house. I get a whiff of myself. I smell like poop. Poop and rubber trees. Lisa doesn't notice.

Lisa's hands are painfully gnarled. Every time she bends over, she must drag her entire body behind her to pick up a doll. I can see her bones under her dress. None of this seems to bother her, as she tells me about her dolls.

"So, this one is Beatrice, this one is Abigail and this one is Hortense." I think to myself, these names...are amazing!!!

I pick up Beatrice, Lisa picks up Hortense. We make them dance together on the perfect lawn. Without looking at each other, or perhaps we are looking at each other through the doll's eyes, I make small talk.

"Is that your grandmother?" I ask.

"Yes, we're going to the library today," she says.

Because of my mother's mental illness and my father's job, I miss out on a lot of activities that are expected experiences for other kids. Instead of reading at the library, I run around the neighborhood terrorizing cats and eating in strange apartments. At six years old, I'm already in the weeds and Lisa is enriching her mind.

The summer months go by. Every time Lisa is in town, playing by herself on the manicured lawn, I step away from my tiny mayoral duties to play with her. I become the runner from the doll tea party to the front porch, getting things from her grandmother to enhance our play time.

School starts in the fall, and Lisa stops visiting as often. I miss my new friend. One day, there is a soft knock at our front door. My mother screams out in a hazy rage, "Who is it?"

"Mrs. Hansen, your neighbor from up the street," an elderly voice says.

My mother tightens her pink fuzzy bathrobe and ties back her hair with a scarf. Suddenly composed, she opens the door, "Hello Mrs. Hansen, what can I do for you?"

"Hello, I wanted to talk to you about your son," she says.

I perk up. I come running down the lopsided stairs and hide behind my mother's robe.

Mrs. Hansen continues, "My granddaughter has an extremely severe case of juvenile rheumatoid arthritis. She has been visiting me for years, but no one ever took an interest in her. I believe her physical limitations scare the other children away. Your son has been the only child on this block who would play with her. He's an extraordinary child. I would like to take him to the library each week with your permission to thank him for his kindness."

My mother, who had been stiff and clearly bracing herself for bad news softens. "Thank you, Mrs. Hansen, this is extremely welcome. I'll make sure Sean knows and is ready for the library when you are ready to take him. Thank you again. Have a good day."

My mother glances behind her and sees me hiding. She winks at me, and then closes the door.

Sean Ewert

Thank God for English Teachers

B y my senior year in high school, my drinking and drugging had bloomed into addiction. I got busted at a party, was locked up in detox, and eventually landed in treatment. Eventually, I got sober.

At seventeen I had to start over. I had been a popular partier, a cocky kid with a quick wit and a smart mouth. That had all been a schtick to cover up the pain and confusion and loneliness of adolescence. Without dope, I felt raw, vulnerable, and exposed. Who was I? What would I be?

Thank God for English teachers. Roger Mahn, my journalism teacher during my senior year at Wayzata High School, spotted what he deemed talent in the sports columns I scratched out for the student newspaper, and he took a personal interest in me. During an independent study with him that year, the conversation in our one-on-one sessions was more likely to turn toward growing as a person than revising a lede paragraph. That's the way he was with all of the students: encouraging them to risk being themselves. He cared about us as people first, and we could tell.

For me, it worked. Roger—as we called him—helped me stay sober my senior year. He kindled an interest in writing. And he inspired me to teach.

He gave me the push that year to start freelancing—at first writing for the community newspaper—and I haven't stopped. More than forty years later, I've written for more than a hundred publications, published ten books, and won a few awards along the way. I also taught high school English for several years and a magazine writing course at the University of Minnesota's journalism school.

Most importantly, I'm still sober. Without his support and influence that first year, my life not only wouldn't have been the same, but it might not have even been anymore.

John Rosengren

This essay first appeared in the anthology, "Thank you, Teacher: Grateful Students Tell the Stories of the Teachers who Changed their Lives" (New World Library, 2016). It is reprinted here with permission from the author.

Audrey

When I retired a few years ago, I was delighted to be able to be of service. One of my volunteer activities is with a hospice where I visit patients' homes once a week. Not doing medical care, just *being* with them. My experiences have been varied: I read Mary Oliver's poetry to one man who was unable to speak due to his advanced Parkinson's Disease, I read the Bible to a former minister, and I played memory games with a 95-year-old woman.

For the last eight months, I have visited Audrey, a 91-year-old British widow who was bedridden, blind in one eye, and had a number of medical issues. Memory loss or dementia were not among them. She was the very definition of the phrase "sharp as a tack". I had an immediate connection with her. She was engaging and charming, despite the pain that her condition caused. She was a wonderful raconteur, telling stories about her childhood in

Britain, about her marriage and two children, and their move to America 50 years ago. Not only did she have a terrific sense of humor, but she was also extremely considerate and kind. Although I was there to provide her comfort and support, I felt that I was the one who benefited from her care and concern. My afternoons with Audrey were the highlight of my week! Sadly, I knew they would come to an end. I just didn't know when.

One afternoon, we were talking about her upcoming birthday. I said, "I hope I live to 92." She looked at me, slightly alarmed, and said, "Meredith! Why?!"

I've always imagined living into my 90s, healthy, just like my mother. Audrey and I didn't continue the conversation beyond her one-word question to me. But I thought about it for days and had a life-changing insight. I like to think that I have lived by the phrase "Be here now". But that's not what I've been doing. I've been projecting into the future when all I really have is now. I finally understood the thought behind her *"Why?!"* I think it was "be careful what you wish for, and appreciate your health and good fortune as long as you have it". Who in their right mind would want to be alive—if blind, terminally ill, and bedridden.

Audrey had no idea that she delivered a random act of kindness to me. But our brief conversation will stay with me for a lifetime. The irony is that I was the one who benefited from *her* kindness.

Her 92nd birthday was shortly after that. She died the following weekend. If I could talk to her now, I would say: Audrey, thank you for letting me into your life as it was ending. I know that you were in pain much of the time, but you never let on. What a gift you gave me: to live my life, no matter how long it is, in the moment. I will miss our Wednesday afternoons and will think of you often.

Meredith Flynn

Danke

(an excerpt from *94 Maidens* by Rhonda Fink-Whitman)

The classroom was vivid and cheerful, decorated wall to wall in student artwork celebrating Israel's upcoming Independence Day. As had become my yearly ritual at Temple B'nai Abraham Religious School in an affluent suburb of Philadelphia, I planted my twenty sixth-grade students in front of an outdated 36-inch television monitor. It was Yom HaShoah, the Annual Day of Remembrance of the Holocaust. This was the time of year I was required to delicately introduce the horrors of the Holocaust to my fresh-faced students who had spent the earlier part of the year focusing on Prayers, Jewish life cycle events, holidays, traditions and Jewish history since the Babylonian era.

This would be the heaviest lesson of the school year. But when I would do a year-end wrap up with the children and ask them what they remembered most from time spent in my classroom, what we learned that had the most impact on them, invariably the majority of the kids would cite this particular lesson.

I peeled open a well-worn white cardboard video box and inserted an old VHS tape into the antiquated machine.

We sat in rows and watched a testimonial, compliments of the Shoah Foundation.

On the TV, an unseen interviewer was asking an elderly woman, in her late 80s with bleached blond hair, large eyeglasses and a thick German accent to describe her captivity in Bergen Belsen.

At the bottom of the screen appeared the name: "Regina Joel Weksler."

"It wasn't a hill at all," Regina described on the tape. "It was bodies, dead bodies, piled one on top of the other..."

The students were riveted by her eyewitness account. I dabbed the corners of my eyes. Although I had seen the tape a hundred times before, and I was in the room the day of the shooting, it still affected me to hear her story. In fact, I was the one responsible for the testimonial being taped having relentlessly begged Regina to record her story, if not for herself, then for posterity—for her grandchildren, of which I was one. My persistence eventually paid off and although Regina had passed away a few years earlier, I was still able to bring her into my classroom, introduce her to a new crop of eager students, and have her help me teach the lessons of the Holocaust.

A couple of the girls sitting on either side of me offered a sympathetic shoulder. I put an arm around each girl and acknowledged them with a maternal smile. These were my kids. Year after year, I formed a bond with these children as if they were my own. Working on TV was fun, but teaching these kids was my passion and educating them Jewishly was rewarding in so many ways. Nothing was more important to me than, as the Rabbi liked to call it, "making Jews."

> *The Interviewer on the video asked, "When you first went into hiding, where did you go?"*
>
> *"To a woman who used to clean our apartment," Regina responded. "And, she took us in."*

I used the remote to pause the video. I had some information I thought the kids might find interesting. "You know," I interrupted. "I actually met the woman who risked her life <u>and</u> her children's lives to hide my mother and grandmother from the Nazis. Would you like to hear that story?"

The students responded with enthusiasm. "Yeah!"

"All right," I said. "Gather round."

The kids moved their chairs to form a semicircle around me.

"When I was in college, I studied for a semester in London. My British cousin decided to take me to Germany to see his mother and meet someone very special..."

BERLIN, 1984

I was only 20 at the time. Tall and hardened, 56-year-old Josef Tymberg brought me into a small, modest flat in a busy, clustered section of the city. I was looking very 80's with my big hair, parachute pants, and denim and red "Michael Jackson Thriller" vest. My collar was up.

On a crisp white sofa, two petite elderly ladies sat smiling and chatting away in German like two twittering little birds. Clearly, they were old friends.

One of the women, familiar at 82, wore a colorful satin patterned dress with coifed red hair and oversized glasses. She had a number tattoo on her left forearm and a permanently deformed right hand; an ever-present reminder of sadistic medical experiments endured at Auschwitz's notorious Block 10, of which she would never speak.

The other, older woman had her grey hair pulled straight back into a tight bun and wore a simple blue and purple floral housedress. An olive green blouse peeked out at her neckline. Her skin was flawless. There were no lines on her 90-year-old face. She was plain but remarkably beautiful.

Joe and I approached the women. They looked at me with wide eyes.

"Mother," Joe said. "It's Rhonda."

I practically mowed down the woman with the red hair.

"Tante Rosa!" I squealed, enormously happy to see Regina's big sister, my great aunt.

"Oye! Rhondala," she said in her thick German accent as she maintained her balance. "I'm so glad Josef brought you here. I haven't seen you since you were a baby!" Rosa had no young people in her life anymore and she gazed lovingly at me as if I was her only hope for the future.

"I have warm regards for you from my mother and grandmother," I told her. She beamed.

Joe led me to the other woman who was smiling brightly.

"Rhonda," he introduced. "This is…"

As I shifted my attention to the elder woman, I suddenly felt swollen with awe and gratitude. I dropped to my knees. Before me sat the most righteous person I would ever meet. I couldn't believe my eyes. My heart pounded. This frail, unassuming old soul had the chutzpah to take on the Third Reich. At this moment I knew what courage was and I would surely never be the same.

"Frau Tietze," I uttered with sheer reverence.

I took her aged hands gently in mine.

All of my feelings bubbled to the top. I had so much to say and it all wanted to gush out at once.

Somehow, none of it seemed sufficient.

> *"It is an honor to meet you. If it weren't for you, I wouldn't be…" I began to rattle on in English.*

Frau Tietze looked confused.

> *"German, leibschen, German!" Tante*

Rosa pleasantly instructed.

"She doesn't speak English," my cousin Joe explained. "Do you know any German?"

I thought about it for a moment.

> *"I know one word, but it's the only word I really need," I told him.*

I looked deeply into Frau Tietze's compassionate blue eyes. I was completely overcome with emotion.

> *"Danke," I choked.*

Frau Tietze smiled even bigger. A tear rolled down her sweet, humble face.

My students were attentively listening to my story. One of my overachievers, Emily, 12, eagerly shot up her hand.

"What does "danke" mean?"

"It's German for "thank you."

They got silent. I saw the need to take a breather.

"Ok, you guys," I blurted. "What do ya say we take five upstairs, then head into the Sanctuary and wait for the family Holocaust program to begin?"

"Ok."

"Cool.

I put my arms out.

"Hugs!" I demanded with a wink.

Happily, the students came over and gave their teacher one serious group hug. I could see that a few of them still had heavy hearts. It was time to lighten the mood.

"Last one up is a moldy bagel!" I announced.

The students froze, unsure whether I was kidding or not. Taking the lead, I dramatically bolted out of the classroom. Feeling somewhat relieved, the kids followed me out in hot, giddy pursuit.

Rhonda Fink-Whitman

***

Danke first appeared as a chapter in the book, 94 Maidens (ITL HAPN, LLC, 2012). It is reprinted here with permission from the author.

The Greatest Act of Kindness

What act of kindness can possibly be greater than saving someone's life? How about bringing someone back from the dead. My name is Ian Carlton, and I am the former dead guy. This is my story.

To fully appreciate the event that changed my life, you must understand the roots. In 1966, at the age of 7-1/2, I attended my very first Major League Baseball game: LA Dodgers vs. NY Mets at Shea Stadium. Turns out, it would be the last time Sandy Koufax would face the Mets. And the Mets beat him up pretty bad that day. In hindsight, I believe this was the reason why Koufax decided to retire. That, along with the fact that he had also given up a homerun to Bob Uecker!

In any event, I fell in love with baseball and made my parents sign me up for the local Little League. The season was already underway, so I had to try out for a position with any team that would take me. Fast forward 55 years, and I am still playing ball. I have not missed a season in between. Baseball, and now softball, is a big part of my life.

On the morning of Sunday, September 27, 2020, I was playing softball in the same league I have been playing in since 1998. With this league, we are usually not playing so late into September. But due to Covid, everything was delayed a couple months as the season did not get underway until late June. Normally, our season is over by the beginning of July.

This particular Sunday was cloudy, overcast and a little cool. It was a crucial game as the winner would get a playoff spot and the loser would be done for the season. I am the pitcher for my team. Bottom of the fifth, score tied at 8-8 and my team is at bat. With one out and a runner on second, it's my turn to hit. I lace a sharp line drive right to the shortstop, so I'm out. I cannot even advance the runner over to third. I trot back to the dugout and sit down on my chair. Due to Covid, we were not allowed to use the benches in the dugout. We had to bring our own beach chair if we wanted to sit. I get into my chair, take a swig of water, and that's it. That is the absolute last thing I remember. Turns out, I had a massive heart attack. And I died on the field.

Now when I say I died, I mean that literally. Later, I was told that my heart was stopped for almost five minutes. I can't even hold my breath for 30 seconds! My team's manager is a dentist who is trained in CPR, but in all his years of practice, he has never had to perform it on anyone. And he was having a difficult time just getting me into position to begin. A commotion began and the young daughter of one of the other players screamed.

This got the attention of one of the players from a different team who was playing on the adjacent field that morning. Turns out, he was an ER doctor from Penn Presbyterian Hospital in Philadelphia. Thinking that someone was hurt, he came over to see if he could help. Little did he know that this was going to be just another day at the office for him.

The ER doc immediately assessed the situation and began performing CPR. As good luck would have it, there was another doctor on the opposing team who would assist him. *911* was called and an ambulance was on its way. In those few minutes in between, the doctors on the field performed CPR and eventually got my heart started once again. When the ambulance finally arrived (approximately 12 minutes after the initial call), they were going to take me to the nearest hospital. However, the ER doctor advised them to take me instead to a different hospital that has a heart specialty facility with a stellar reputation.

The ER doctor also specified the particular heart surgeon he wanted on the case. Clinging to life, I was now on my way to Our Lady of Lourdes Hospital. The event was so overwhelming that the two games going on at the field were postponed until the following week. No one wanted to play ball after all that just happened.

To make matters even more complicated, no one had told my wife and family about the venue change to Lourdes. They were told I was being taken to Virtua Hospital in

Marlton, NJ. When they got there, they were informed I had not arrived yet, but I was actually on the ambulance that just pulled in. Imagine their shock when it turned out that it was not me! Eventually, the hospital staff was able to figure out where I was, and my family was able to get over there to meet up with me.

After finally getting me stabilized, the heart surgeon explained to my wife what occurred and what was needed to be done. I finally woke up two and a half days later to learn of the events that took place, and what was yet to come. I needed a quadruple bypass. Because of the length of time that I was dead, the surgeon explained that there was only about a six percent chance of success but without it, there was no chance for survival.

He went on to explain that even if the operation were successful, there was a high probability that I would have either a physical or mental handicap to have to deal with. This was due to the length of time I was dead. The operation was performed on Friday, October 2, and was completely successful. My heart was rebuilt and was going to be fine. We had to wait and see if there were going to be any residual effects.

The next day, I was in the recovery room when my son came in to see me. I was awake but completely out of it, and it looked like I was sleeping. He saw all the wires and gauges and monitors I was hooked up to and was looking at everything, taking it all in. Mustering up all the strength I had at the time, I said to him, "What are you doing? Looking for the plug?" At that moment, both he and my wife realized that my brain was fine. That would have been the exact same obnoxious, sarcastic comment that I would have made under normal circumstances.

I learned to walk again while still in the hospital. I went to cardiac rehab upon my release. And I was able to finally lose those last 10 pounds of ugly, stubborn fat without resorting to cutting off my head. (A credit to Rodney Dangerfield for that line.) I went back to work full-time three months after the surgery. I was present for the birth of my second grandchild. And most importantly, I was back on the field for another season of softball. And I actually had a pretty good season.

All this was made possible by the unbridled kindness of a couple of doctors who had wanted nothing more than to play ball in their regular Sunday morning softball league. Had I been any place else when I collapsed, I would not be here writing these words now. I don't know what the proper protocol is to say *thank you* to these gentlemen who saved my life.

I saw the ER doc earlier this season when my team played his team for the first time since I *died*. We hugged, and I told him "I just don't know how to say *Thank you.*" He said to me that as a doctor, there is no greater reward than to see a patient who didn't look like he was going to make it not only recover but resume his life where he left off.

It was once famously said that there is no crying in baseball. I'm a very emotional person and I cried twice this past softball season. The first time was when the ER doc said those words to me about the greatest reward. The second time came in the first game of the season. Upon stepping into the batter's box for my first at bat, the opposing team's players each took one step forward and simultaneously tipped their cap to me. That's about as high an honor as you can receive.

My life was saved, and I was able to make a full and complete recovery because of the kindness and comradery of the people who play in my softball league. Playing in a league that is stacked with professionals was the key to my survival. Let that be a lesson to you if you are in my age category and still want to play ball.

Another great takeaway from this episode is that I now have something that keeps my wife at bay. You see, for many years now, she has been after me to retire from softball. "Doesn't it take longer and longer for the aches and pains to go away after every game?" is what she says to me. Now, when she gives me a hard time for playing ball, I tell her this. "Honey, if I weren't playing softball on that fateful Sunday morning, I would be dead."

Astonishingly, that seems to shut down her retirement demands.

Ian Carlton

Meant to Be

A lot goes on in our lives, and sometimes we can find it hard to step back and take note of various acts of kindness. Whether it is for me and my family, or in fact for anyone that I know, it can be challenging to remember that which is done and shows kindness. Recently, when asked if I had any stories reflecting on this, I simply couldn't recount any such incidents, and felt like a crummy person for not being able to come up with even one story. And then, just three days ago, two acts of kindness tied to the same event fell in my lap. It was fate.

The story starts with my daughter starting her career with a new job in New York City. Although she started working remotely, her team set up a day for her to come to the city to meet everyone, and to partake in a team dinner after work. She parked at a station in central Jersey, took the train into the city and had what she described as a fantastic day meeting her new team. After work, they enjoyed dinner and some drinks, and it was a very special day. Until it wasn't.

As she got back to Penn Station for her trip home, she suddenly realized that she no longer had her purse. Yep, the purse that contained her money, car keys and driver's license. At this point, it was after 10:30 p.m. and she was now in New York City with no ability to get home. Cue the panicky phone call. My wife and I quickly decide we will drive to NYC to pick her up and hop in my car. By this point it is starting to approach 11 p.m.

We give our daughter instructions to find a crowded place to sit at Penn Station until we could arrive there. (Fortunately, it is New York City, so there is always a crowd there, no matter the time.) While heading toward the New Jersey Turnpike, it hits me that I have some standing with Marriott thanks to years of traveling and staying at their hotels. I decide to call one that is near Penn Station. I talk to an employee named Daniel and explain the situation. He is understanding and caring but also has strict guidelines he has to adhere to, which make sense: they cannot check-in anyone without a photo ID. So, my gut gets a little tighter as I am afraid this plan will not work. But this is where Act of Kindness Number One comes in.

Daniel tells me that he will do everything in his power and within company guidelines to make sure my daughter is safe. And he starts thinking of ideas that can help her. Most importantly, he asks us to tell her to come to the lobby, ask for him and he will watch after her until this gets resolved. We mention that we have her passport at home and together conclude that if we go home, scan it and send it to him via email, he can use that to check her in. It's now close to 11:30 p.m. and she has a place to stay for the night. My wife and I had only driven for about fifteen minutes at this point, instead of the normal two hours to get to New York City. Act of Kindness Number One is in the books.

As this is resolving, Act of Kindness Number Two occurs. While I am on the phone with Daniel, my daughter messages my wife that someone has found her purse. Not only did he find it but looked at her ID and messaged her through Facebook, saying that he had it and wanted to return it. It had fallen onto the street when she left her Uber ride at Penn Station.

So, some random person finds her purse, with ID, credit cards, car keys and other items, and does the right thing. He goes out of his way to get in touch with her in order to return it, giving her his cell phone number. This man had worked a very long day and was heading home on a train after 11:30 p.m. She called him and he committed to keeping her purse safe, but he was already on his way home. He asked her if she could meet him at Penn Station around 6:30 a.m., when he would be back the next day for work. Which she did, and she got her purse back with all contents intact. The only thing he would accept from her as a *thank-you* was just that, a verbal "Thank you."

So, there you have it. After struggling to think of acts of kindness, two such acts happened around the same event, and everything worked out for the best in the end. My daughter was safe, with all her personal possessions still in hand, and my faith in the goodness of people was restored. Overall, a great night!

Rich Glass

Showing Faith

For about 10 years, I had been working for a company that sold computer solutions to municipalities throughout the state of New Jersey. It was a small company of about 30 employees, for which my job was primarily computer application training and support. I was in my early 40s and had three kids. I was contemplating making a career move and had just gone back to a community college to pursue my associate degree.

With three kids and a full-time job, I could only manage to take one course per semester, so pursuing a college education was a slow-going process. I stayed with it, as I knew that without a college degree my options would be limited.

One night, my husband and I went out to dinner and happened to run into old friends of ours that we had not seen in over five years. We joined them at their table and during the conversation, I mentioned that I was thinking of looking for a new job.

My old friend Connie was working for a company called Electronic Data Systems (EDS). EDS was a huge consulting firm out of Plano, Texas and they were looking for people to join their Organizational Development (OD) team on a five-year project at Cigna, which was based in New Jersey. She asked what I was doing at the computer company, and when I mentioned *training*, she suggested I apply for a position conducting and managing training at EDS.

Now, I had only worked for *small* companies throughout my career and had no idea what OD even was. I had conducted one-on-one training but had never been in front of a room full of people before. I did a little research before my panel interview with five EDS managers and was shocked when I was offered the position.

Most members of the OD team were not only college-educated but also had their PhDs. Here I was, a high school grad surrounded by PhD professionals, now working for a huge global company. I later realized that Connie had put great faith in my potential and ability to work hard to get up-to-speed quickly. She stuck her neck out to recommend me when I did not have the qualifications. At least not on paper.

I worked at EDS for five years, conducting soft-skills training for classes of 15–20 people in New Jersey and Connecticut. During that time, I was also asked to join their corporate team, for which I conducted training across the

United States. I doubled my salary from what I was making at the computer company. And after leaving EDS, I was hired by Lockheed Martin, where I tripled my initial salary. I continued to pursue my education and graduated at age 52 with a degree in Organizational Development. I went into semi-retirement from Lockheed Martin at the age of 60 and fully retired at 64.

Putting faith in others and going to bat for them is, to me, an act of kindness. Without Connie's faith in me, I would never have been hired by EDS and achieved a degree in Organizational Development, nor been hired at Lockheed Martin. In addition, I would probably not have been able to enjoy retirement by age 64. Connie's act of kindness set me in a direction that I would have never pursued and enabled me to have a fulfilling career and a financially secure retirement.

Pat Kelly

Scrambled Eggs

I had a big day planned. It was Monday and I got to the office early so I could hit the road by 8:30. I had appointments set for 9:00 and 10:15, and then planned to do some cold-calling to fill out the morning. It was a beautiful, late-summer day with a slight hint of autumn in the air and I was excited about my prospects. You know, *carpe diem* and all that other simplistic, motivational-speaker jibber-jabber. I'd been trying for months to get an appointment with the person I was seeing at 9:00; he was a legitimate prospect who could potentially spend a great deal of money.

When I arrived fifteen minutes early, I was told by the receptionist he was running about fifteen minutes late and to please have a seat. I sat there reading and stewing until 9:30 when I finally asked if she had heard anything yet. She smiled and said she hadn't, but it shouldn't be too much longer. Finally, at 9:45, I left.

Peeved to the max.

I got to my 10:15 early since it was only a ten-minute drive, which worked out fine because that appointment's assistant was in the process of calling me to let me know my meeting was cancelled. Apparently, some emergency with one of her kid's braces was the excuse *du jour*, and I was having none of it. The assistant was one of those disturbingly bubbly people who would irritate me on the best of days, and her joyfully beaming sweet talk was only exacerbating the situation.

She was so damned happy while I was so damned unhappy. My irritation and disappointment were thinly veiled and I probably wasn't very pleasant to the animated, Nicholsonesque joker from hell. I was in no mood to be nice—not on this morning, not the way it was going so far.

I drove down the street and came to a red light. Across the intersection was a giant beer store, and next to it was a diner. The beer store wasn't open yet, so I went into the diner and ordered breakfast. I ate my eggs and read the paper, and, as I was finishing, the waitress walked over and said, "There were two ladies sitting at that table," pointing across the room.

The next thing she said ripped a hole in my isolated universe of alienation and self-pity. "They paid for your breakfast."

"What! They paid for my breakfast?" I repeated, trying to sort out the conflicting freight trains of surprise and suspicion colliding in my head. "What do you mean they paid for my breakfast?"

"They asked for your check and paid it. That's all I know," the waitress offered in a calming tone, trying to help me through this unexpected experience.

"Who were they?" I asked, but the waitress had no idea.

"Maybe it was just a random act of kindness," she said, giving me a tender smile as she hurried away to resume her responsibilities.

I'm sure I would have recognized the women if I knew them. What did they want with me? Whatever they wanted, they sure weren't getting any since I had no idea who they were. Did I look like I needed a free meal, like I should be standing on an off-ramp with a sign reading "Will manifest a look of complete bewilderment for food"? I was having serious trouble wrapping my brain around this one. I understood being stood up for appointments and discourteous customers—I'd been dealing with that type of thoughtlessness for 35 years—but this was an altogether different animal.

Why was this happening to me? Why were they messing with my neat, little world? Who would subject me to such pain and torment?

I decided to confront the cashier. I would ask her if the women paid with a credit card, and if so, would she please give me the name on the card. I wasn't sure she would, but it was worth a chance to end this downright disturbing dilemma. As I waited in line behind another customer paying his check, I caught a glimpse of myself in the mirror behind the cashier's stand. I looked demonic. My brow was furrowed and my eyes were narrowed in consternation; my lips were twisted in a look of barely suppressed anger. It was a frightening and shocking sight.

What was I thinking?

Somebody did something nice for me, for no discernible reason and with no apparent ulterior motive, and here I stood, ready to fight to the death, to annihilate and banish these seemingly kind, good Samaritans from the face of the earth. My wrath was palpable.

And wholly misplaced.

I got out of there quickly and sat in my car staring at a scantily clad Betty Boop dancing inside the fluid globe of the suicide knob attached to my steering wheel, thinking about what had just happened and trying to figure out what was going on with me. I'd let myself go to a very bad place, from my first disappointment of the morning until a generous gesture of gentle humanity brought out the resentment and guilt that resides in all our souls; in most of us it's kept safely under control in the dungeons of our deepest psyches, while in others is easily brought to the surface with the slightest provocation. And from whichever position you come, it's always your choice.

I thought I'd learned that lesson before, many times over, but some disciplines take constant vigilance and caution as *we few, we happy few* navigate the labyrinth of self-doubt and narcissistic pride on the precarious course of exchanging commodities or services for monetary consideration.

The profession of sales can be one bitch of a mistress!

"Driving in my car, smoking my cigar " (I don't really smoke but I love that Jack Bruce lyric), I couldn't turn it off; my mind kept coming back to how I'd let myself get "tangled up in blue" (a Dylan lyric I also happen to love and aren't we having a swell time playing *Name That Tune?*). I thought of Zig Ziglar and one of his legendary parables I'd recently been reintroduced to on YouTube.

The video is called *Attitude Makes All the Difference*, and I highly recommend watching it if for no other reason than to catch Ziglar at his animated and entertaining best. You may find Zig a wee bit old-fashioned (and if you don't, then you most likely didn't have to Google any of the references in the proceeding paragraphs), but his message is timeless and as valuable today as it was when he first set out peddling his homespun, salt-of-of-the-earth philosophy. I won't ruin it for you by retelling the story (I couldn't do it justice, anyway), but the message is that you have all the power to control how the world treats you.

Surprise, surprise. You're in charge. It all comes down to your attitude, like everything else, and that's not such a big surprise after all.

But "it don't come easy" (yes, another tattered and frayed lyric from days gone by, delivered by the least formidable of the most formidable, Richard Starkey, and have fun with that one on Google). You have to work at it and work at it every day. A good attitude does not magically appear with the wave of a wand and a puff of smoke, but comes from preparation and execution.

It's my hard-earned belief that success is not the result of a good attitude, but a good attitude is the result of success. And the only way to achieve success is to work hard and work smart. If you do that, you will be successful. It's that simple.

And just as simple, a good attitude will follow like night follows day.

You can take that to the bank.

And one more thing. Note to The Big Guy: Next time you're gracious enough to visit me with a random act of kindness, could you please give me a heads up. I was going to have the eggs Benedict that morning, but I didn't want to go the extra three bucks.

Thank you.

Richard Plinke

(Reprinted with permission from Richard Plinke, author of *From the Jaws of the Dragon*)

Roadhouse Blues

It was Mother's Day. I was feeling a bit down. I decided to take myself to Texas Roadhouse for dinner. Armed with a book to read, I gave my name and was told I'd have a 45-minute wait. I picked a bench in the sun.

There was a gentleman on the other end. I commenced reading my book and checked my phone for a text about every 10 minutes or so. While I was reading, the man's wife joined him. Not a big deal for me. I was, as usual, engrossed in the book I was reading.

Next thing I know, a couple who knew the people on my bench came by. I asked if they wanted me to move. I was met with a chorus of *nos*. The two women began to talk over me. It was annoying, but there was no longer any place to move. I attempted to go back to reading. Then the grandkids showed up. They also knew the other couple.

A son or son-in-law stood behind me, blocking the sun. Which made it difficult to read. I got lucky. My wait was only 30 minutes, and now I could go inside. The hostess seated me and left burned buns and cinnamon butter on the table.

The waitress took my drink order and I asked for an appetizer. She brought the drink and wished me a happy Mother's Day *if I was one*. I told her I am a mom, but we were in Kentucky, and my daughter lived in Michigan. They had to repair my drink as it was terrible, and she brought my appetizer.

The tables all around me were filled with families. I ate my appetizer and discovered fresh rolls on the table. I continued to read and munch until my dinner was served. I cut up my steak and picked the book back up to finish my meal.

I was almost done when my waitress arrived and told me to take my time and enjoy the rest of my meal as a group who had been across from me—and a table up—had paid my dinner bill. They did not like to see me eating alone on Mother's Day.

The gesture brought me to tears. It was not expected. I had been discouraged at the beginning of my meal, but the waitress came through to make it enjoyable. Then, to have someone pay the bill! I will forever be grateful for their kindness. I often look for ways to brighten the days of others. I am shocked and humbled when someone goes out of their way to brighten mine.

Rebecka Vigus

Artistic Praise and Utility Poles

L ife was tough for everyone during quarantine, whether the pandemic imposed mental, social, or physical struggles. However, it was also a time to find new passions: for me, that hobby was art. During the Covid-19 outbreak, students internationally had to take their classes virtually. While many did not put in much effort for special area classes, I found art assignments enjoyable and inspiring rather than a chore.

We had a student-teacher, whose name I will not reveal, during this particular marking period. She gave us a project to create our own album covers as if we were music artists. It was pretty lenient and low stress considering both the pandemic and the kids who weren't Vincent van Goghs. I, however, was enlightened by this idea of creating album art and started immediately. I began during our "lunch break," which seemed unnecessary considering kids just ate during Google Meets, but I highly appreciated it. I took pictures of myself outside, one in particular of me reaching one arm as if my life depended on it. Later, I edited that photo onto utility power poles outside my house to look like I was hanging from the wires.

What seemed silly all came together with some editing. I made three more *album covers*, taking inspiration from some of my favorite music artists and other popular ones. I was probably going for an indie singer-songwriter look using low exposure and cool tones. Satisfied, I submitted my work, and left a private comment for the student-teacher explaining why I decided to overachieve in doing four covers instead of one. It went along the lines of me enjoying the assignment and how I had multiple ideas to express and share. She at first replied with a "No problem! I'm happy you enjoyed the assignment; I'm grading them next week", an anticipated answer.

A month or two later, when it came time for the student teacher to leave and the marking period to end, she left another comment on my project. I was curious, considering it was now an old assignment, and it had already been graded. I did not expect the kind words and praise she wrote to me that day, especially months after the assignment had been graded. She wrote, "I am seriously so proud of these album covers. You have an eye for aesthetics. I would buy any of these.".

This simple comment made my day and made me much more confident in my artistic ability. I still think about that comment today; she probably didn't realize how much that meant to me. I have no intention of becoming an artist, but the artistic field has always been one of my passions and strengths. In my childhood, I pretty much did it all: singing, dancing, visual art, writing, etc.

People don't realize how much a compliment like that can raise a person's confidence in their work. You never know what people are going through. A compliment, primarily focusing on one of their passions or abilities, can brighten someone's day. No matter how small it may seem, it can end up being significant to the receiver. No matter how cliché it sounds, treating others with kindness goes a long way.

Katie Sullivan

Compassionate Voices

While hitchhiking on an interstate outside of Orlando, Florida, my thoughts were focused on how depressing life had become. Standing over a roadkill and speaking to myself, absorbed in self-pity, I was making the effort to convince myself that circumstances could be much worse. Thoughts directed at G-d were expressed as, "Take me if you must."

How had life come to this?

University studies included work internship periods with responsibilities in the city of Orlando. Friends and school were halfway across the state in the town of Melbourne, Florida. Routine had become the normal back-and-forth on weekends between a rented room in Melbourne and one rented close to work in Orlando.

Transportation options had become extremely limited. Hitchhiking was often choice mode for getting to places because the State of Florida had pulled my driver's license for one year. Admittedly, my driving had displayed a lack of responsible behavior, but the majority of points assessed against my license were the result of an incident which took place one night after working late.

Two co-workers decided that they would challenge each other to a race. While my car was not at all in participation, police had arrived and issued tickets to all drivers. My day in court turned out to be a complete farce as an officer testified that my white Ford had led the race.

The judge was not interested in the location of my auto or that my car was, indeed, blue. Speaking my mind to the bench, I said, "If it does not matter how fast my car was traveling, or that my car was a quarter mile behind ... nor what color is my car ... then I guess I am deserving of all your charges". The judge did not take kindly to my candid commentary and slammed his gavel.

During this time, my grandparents were hospitalized with life-threatening illnesses. Prior to the internet, there was just the dependence for information on long-distance phone calls. It was heart-wrenching to realize the absence of those so critical in the formation of my life. So many years have passed and, still today, even the mention of my grandfather will bring me to tears.

Also at that time, the most beautiful girl of my college beach town—according to my standards—had been dating me for several months. This girl set my lifetime high bar for beauty, and for a short while she was my girl. Her regrettable decision to return to her ex-boyfriend had truly hurt my heart. Life would be full of disappointments, yet this one had left a mark.

Concurrently, a dear friend was going through his own challenges. He could stroke laughter from anyone around him. We initially lived together in a dorm. After months of knowing each other, we found ourselves drinking in a pub with a visitor, who pointed out that a Jew and an Arab getting along so well was something extraordinary. We honestly had never considered any of that, and both shook our heads.

He was Syrian, and he would proudly clarify that when told by anyone to act *serious*. Arab bread for us was a special treat. We experienced many years of maturing together. He once diagnosed me as oversexed and undersupplied. It was his comical approach that had me nearly bitten when reaching my hand halfway into a bucket as he questioned me about a type of snake. In a nervous laugh, he followed with, "Yes, but what *kind* of rattlesnake?".

Depression must be recognized; as well, it is important to realize that it does pass. My beloved friend went into a profound depression. Other friends would joke that he had become a plant. He became lost so deep in his thoughts and had asked me to discuss matters. The painful truth is that my self-centered impression at the time was that he wanted to talk about issues concerning *me*.

Therefore, my reaction was to avoid any such conversations. My thought was that it was not a problem for me, as this would all be in the past. He told me that he would be making a trip home to New York. As comeback to my envious remark that it must be nice to be able to travel on a whim, his philosophical response was that anything is possible if you make it so. He did travel after a delayed attempt and never returned. He ended his life with a gun, away at the home of his parents.

Take me if you must. Life had become so overwhelmingly negative.

One significantly memorable experience of being touched by an act of kindness happened during this very low point in my life along the interstate. An observant older couple had seen my depressed posture through the rain and made an extended effort to circle back to give me a lift. Miles separate exits along this highway, and it was certainly no easy task for them to make this costly return in the other direction in the hope that maybe they could find me. They were kind people and spoke proudly of their commitment to G-d. My best possible recollection after all these years is that the gentleman was a religious pastor with a loving wife at his side. Soft tones of their voices were sounding full of compassion and most definitely not as lecture. Exact words spoken during conversations unfortunately cannot be remembered. However, this understanding couple left a powerful impact as if they had been appointed by G-d to get me out of the weather.

Later, in middle-age years, my former love interest sought me out through social media, and we once again had each other in our lives. Fortunately, she met my absolutely incredible wife and kids who held pleasant feelings for her. She passed of cancer, but not before giving closure to her chapter of my life.

Acts of kindness by others can be spiritually uplifting, even sometimes life-changing. Disappointingly, they would risk the loss of our appreciation if they were all so commonplace. Hopefully, everyone has come upon a multitude of such experiences.

Thank you for allowing me to share my personal story.

Mitchell Tiger

A Cornucopia of Kindness Quotes

I believe that acts and words of kindness surround us daily. We also have access to a wealth of quotations about the crucial importance of kindness in our lives. These inspiring quotes are derived from a variety of sources, including academia, the entertainment world, literature, philosophy, and even politics. Yes, even politics. What follows is not meant to be a definitive list, but I hope you will enjoy the 36 quotes that I have included here. Many of these quotations were compiled on rd.com (Thank you, *Reader's Digest*.)

No act of kindness, no matter how small, is ever wasted. —Aesop

Whatever possession we gain by our sword cannot be sure or lasting, but the love gained by kindness and moderation is certain and durable. — Alexander the Great

Continue to be who and how you are, to astonish a mean world with your acts of kindness. Continue to allow humor to lighten the burden of your tender heart. — Maya Angelou

Go and love someone exactly as they are. And then watch how quickly they transform into the greatest, truest version of themselves. When one feels seen and appreciated in their own essence, one is instantly empowered. — Wes Angelozzi

It is the characteristic of the magnanimous man to ask no favor but to be ready to do kindness to others. — Aristotle

To err on the side of kindness is seldom an error. — Liz Armbruster

Always be a little kinder than necessary. — James M. Barrie

When words are both true and kind, they can change the world. — Buddha

Sometimes it takes only one act of kindness and caring to change a person's life. — Jackie Chan

Be kind whenever possible. It is always possible. — Dalai Lama, the 14th.

Love and kindness are never wasted. They always make a difference. They bless the one who receives them, and they bless you, the giver. — Barbara De Angelis

Carry out a random act of kindness, with no expectation of reward, safe in the knowledge that one day someone might do the same for you. — Diana, Princess of Wales

A single act of kindness throws out roots in all directions, and the roots spring up and make new trees. — Amelia Earhart

You cannot do kindness too soon, for you never know how soon it will be too late. — Ralph Waldo Emerson

The words of kindness are more healing to a drooping heart than balm or honey. — Sarah Fielding

Kindness begins with the understanding that we all struggle. — Charles Glassman

For attractive lips, speak words of kindness. — Audrey Hepburn

Practice random kindness and senseless acts of beauty. — Anne Herbert

When I was young, I admired clever people. Now that I am old, I admire kind people. — Abraham Joshua Heschel

Kindness can become its own motive. We are made kind by being kind. — Eric Hoffer

Because that's what kindness is. It's not doing something for someone else because they can't, but because you can. —Andrew Iskander

A part of kindness consists in loving people more than they deserve. — Joseph Joubert

Do things for people not because of who they are or what they do in return, but because of who you are. — Harold S. Kushner

Kindness is the only service that will stand the storm of life and not wash out. It will wear well and will be remembered long after the prism of politeness or the complexion of courtesy has faded away. — Abraham Lincoln

A kind gesture can reach a wound that only compassion can heal. — Steve Maraboli

Never doubt that a small group of thoughtful, committed citizens can change the world. Indeed, it is the only thing that ever has. — Margaret Mead

Spread love everywhere you go. Let no one ever come to you without leaving happier. — Mother Teresa

Kind words do not cost much. Yet they accomplish much. — Blaise Pascal

Human kindness has never weakened the stamina or softened the fiber of a free people. — Franklin D. Roosevelt

What wisdom can you find that is greater than kindness? —Jean-Jacques Rousseau

When you callously ignore the suffering of others, you lose the capacity to share their happiness, too. — Albert Schweitzer

Wherever there is a human being, there is an opportunity for a kindness. — Lucius Annaeus Seneca

You can accomplish by kindness what you cannot by force. — Publilius Syrus

Do your little bit of good where you are; it's those little bits of good put together that overwhelm the world. — Desmond Tutu

Kindness is the golden chain by which society is bound together. — Johann Wolfgang von Goethe

Kindness is the light that dissolves all walls between souls, families, and nations. — Paramahansa Yogananda

ACT Four

◊ ◊ ◊

"Kindness is the language which the deaf can hear and the
blind can see."

Mark Twain

Wrestling With Kindness

I don't spend much time on social media. I'll occasionally peek in to see if anyone I know has anything interesting to say, or I'll eavesdrop on the latest political rants. For the most part, though, I'm a social media ghost.

A few years back, however, a name from the past caught my eye under one of those "people you might know" suggestions. It was an old classmate from high school named Graham, a guy I hadn't seen in many years. I can't say Graham and I were besties in high school, but we were very friendly and after graduation, we bumped into each other several times over the years at various events. We always struck up a conversation and it was always nice to see him.

So when his name popped up on my social media feed, I really did want to say hello. The truth is, I had some unfinished business with my old classmate, and I wanted to tell him something: That he was responsible in many ways for changing my life, for changing my outlook on life, for allowing me to recognize that there is good in people. Maybe not all people, but some.

A little background:

I always identified with those fish-out-of-water tales (*Karate Kid*, anyone?) because while growing up, we moved constantly. I attended three elementary schools, two middle schools, and two high schools … in three states. Twice, I changed schools in the middle of the year. I know from experience that the new kid on the block is always a target: Even the wimpiest kids got their licks in because, well, they could. If you were new and completely unknown, you were fair game for all.

One example: While in middle school, the gym teacher, in his infinite wisdom, allowed the students to pick sides for kickball. I was wearing a T-shirt with a shark decal from the movie *Jaws*. Of course, when the final pick came around, yours truly still hadn't been selected. An argument broke out between the team captains. "I did not pick *Jaws*," one "captain" insisted. "Yes, you did, you picked *Jaws*!" "I did *not* pick *Jaws*!" he shot back. And it went back and forth until both made it clear that I was not welcome on either team. Finally, I just walked away and sat alone by the racquetball court.

Another occasion: In ninth grade, I struck up a friendship with a very pretty sophomore named Pam. We had gotten to know one another through CB radio, the social media outlet of the mid-1970s. We were chatting one day before classes and one of Pam's equally pretty classmates walked past, pointed at me and said, "Pam? You can do better than that!" OK, that was bad enough, but check out Pam's reply: "What, are you crazy? He's not my boyfriend! You must be high!"

Talk about a one-two knockout combination. Ouch!

When I moved to Pennsylvania for 10th grade, I enrolled at the local Catholic high school. Not because Mom had suddenly found the Lord, but because my two cousins attended the school. I was the new kid again, but finally I would at least know someone. It helped a little, but both cousins were in different grades, so I would have to get to know the kids in my class on my own.

Shortly after the school year began—in gym class, of course—a couple of jocks were going around the gymnasium floor recruiting kids for the wrestling team. Leading the mission was a popular jock named Graham, and I was convinced that this recruiting effort was nothing more than a trap to make the new kid look like an idiot.

Graham made his way to me and grabbed me by the shoulder and asked my name. "C'mon, Joe we need bodies," he said. I told him I had no experience with wrestling, but he insisted, "No problem, we'll make a wrestler out of you, no problem!" He summoned the gym teacher, who also happened to be the wrestling coach. Graham assured him I was a capable recruit and the coach invited me to join the team. I remained skeptical, but I agreed to give wrestling a try. Practices would begin in about a month and I figured that was plenty of time for them to forget about me.

Fast-forward a few weeks from the gym-class encounter. Our English class took on a project involving mass media and its effect on modern life. The teacher gave the 20 or so students the option of working in groups or handling the project individually. Only one student decided to do it alone: me. The teacher double-checked and offered to assign me to a group, but I said no, I'm okay working on my own.

Gathered in the group directly to my left were four students, with Graham sitting right in the middle. I wasn't paying much attention until I could hear them murmuring something like, "Let's ask him."

"Hey, Joe," Graham said. I pretended not to hear him at first. A kid named Mike also tried to get my attention. They knew I wasn't deaf, so I gave it an, "Oh, you're talking to me?" Graham and Mike both asked something along the lines of, "How come you're working on this alone?" I told them I didn't mind; I work well on my own. "Well, you're welcome to join our little group," Graham said. "We need all the help we can get." All agreed, motioning me to turn my desk around and join them.

What followed was something I'd never experienced. Questions about who I am, where I'm from, how I wound up in Pennsylvania, how I wound up at a Catholic high school. What was public school like? One kid knew my older cousin from the ice hockey team. They were genuinely looking to get to know me. After the small talk, we were assigned tasks. Since I told them I was something of a current-events geek, I was chosen to delve into the news.

A few days later, the group gathered again to go over our work. I can still see Mike looking at what I'd submitted and nodding. "Okay, this is good!" Graham followed with, "Told ya, you picked the right group!" We had to do an oral presentation about a week later and I nailed it. Graham gave me a thumbs-up after I spoke.

So many little moments have stayed with me. Graham might have been popular, but he was approachable. One day, a bunch of students were talking about the movie *Slap Shot*. Graham recited a line from the movie, and I shot back with another one. Before I knew it, we were going back and forth with our favorite lines and cracking up. We even moved to a couple other movies we'd both seen, mimicking the dialogue. I wasn't being ignored. It was liberating.

I eventually made some friends over the following three years, and Graham was always available for a chat. I never became a star wrestler (Graham did), but participating with that team remains the highlight of my high school years. I only did it because Graham encouraged me to do so.

So, my old classmate Graham definitely fell under the category of "people you may know." I hit the friend-request button and dashed off a little note to my old friend.

Here's a summary of what I wrote:

"I never told you this, but I think it's important for you to know. I arrived at our school my sophomore year after spending my first year of high school in Florida. I was a complete stranger in a new school with no friends. To this day, four decades later, I always remembered how you made it a point to be welcoming and friendly to me. Little things in life make such a big difference. You were a very popular kid with an athletic pedigree, yet you made it a point to say to me, *Yo, welcome to the club.* I never forgot that, and I thought it was important for you to know that all these years later a couple of acts of kindness on your part meant the world to me ... you were a role model long before that term became popular. Life can get you down every now and then, but just know how much I appreciated those acts of friendship. Funny thing is, you might not even remember them. But I do. Your kindness had a lifelong impact on me."

The poet Maya Angelou famously said, "I've learned that people will forget what you said, people will forget what you did, but people will never forget how you made them feel." I would make only one slight adjustment to those great words. I can remember just about everything that was ever said to me, both kind and unkind. I remember exactly what those kids who referred to me as "Jaws" said. I remember exactly what they looked like, I can hear their voices. Meanwhile, I wonder if they remember me? Probably not.

I remember the exact words that pretty teenager used, and I remember Pam's reply. I can still see their faces. I can still hear their voices. I can recall just about every cruel, insulting and demeaning word ever said to me. Vividly. After more than four decades, I remember how Pam's friend made me feel. I've often wondered if that girl is aware of the impact of that little throwaway line. I've wondered if she has children of her own, and whether she ever had to comfort them at any point because some rotten kid made them feel like crawling into a hole. I wonder how she would feel if she knew that her one-sentence comment had left a permanent scar.

But … I also remember the kind words. I remember the names of the four guys from that mass media project. I remember their questions. I remember, because they made me feel welcome.

Graham, by the way, replied to my note. He acknowledged that he, indeed, was unaware of the impact of his kindness, and that he was grateful that I had reminded him. He made a lifelong impression on someone with his words, his acts, his kindness.

Speaking carries with it a great responsibility. A kick in the groin hurts, really hurts, but the physical pain goes away. The reason for the kick stays with you. When we speak, we would do well to carefully consider the words we use because they can and will leave permanent marks, both good and bad.

Joe Berkery

City Streets

The girl walked on the city streets, and though the sun wove her fingers throughout the dense crowd and cast her warmth on every street, the girl still felt like a shadow to the group of people chattering excitedly amongst themselves beside her. Alone and not alone.

When they were first introduced, she had acted perfectly and affably as she always did publicly, saying the proper things at the opportune time, smiling and laughing appropriately whenever it was needed. They had smiled at her, welcomed her into their group, and brought her into their fold. But this time she had tried too hard to be liked by this group of people, and as the day went on, too quickly did the sociable manner drain her mind and tug at the fraying edges of her heart until she retired slowly back into the shell of her head, looking past the people, the buildings, the streets, past everything.

Again, the girl bitterly remarked to herself, peripherally observing how they traded warm smiles and laughs as she looked straight ahead. *You have done it again.*

Even the passersby tugged at her, pulling her away like a loose thread from the cuff of a sweater; somehow the rest of them managed to stay together in a line, shoulder-to-shoulder, and eventually the girl surrendered, letting herself be carried behind the group where the waves caught at her more strongly. Standing beside them, where the dark had merely lapped at her ankles, teasing her feet to take a step, and another, and another into the deep, in the midst of the crowd cresting waves now threatened to pull her under.

The girl would be lying if she told herself she did not care so much (but she still tells herself that as she rolls her shoulders back, raises her chin, hardens her eyes even as her heart whispers insinuatingly). She knew it was because she did not try hard enough, did not want it enough, and was not enough for anybody with her reticent nature and the inherent need to be quiet and alone, though the satisfaction of solitude rarely quelled the voice of the little demon (who was actually a little girl) who screamed "unloved! unloved! unloved!" repeatedly behind her eyes.

As she thinks this and much more, the backs of the people she was supposed to be with have receded farther from view and the waves have already come over her eyes and she can no longer see the stars. The tides that are of her making render her immobile and her feelings spiral like a staircase that she tumbles down and down on into an oblivion—

—that fades back into what it was before it became nothing as she feels a hand that gives her own hand a firm squeeze.

It is the girl from before, with the kind eyes, she thinks, seeing not a starless sky but the sun and the bustling city streets again. And this girl leads her forward, parting through the crowds with ease, this girl's hand gently gripping hers.

When their group comes back into sight again, they both stay behind. This girl throws a glance back every once in a while, as if to make sure she is still here, if she is still anchored. When the crowd thickens in busy streets, this girl grips her hand again and pulls her beside herself. They do not talk. They do not feel the need to because the silence feels as delicious as if they had been talking.

Isabella Zhang

Anonymous Kindness

In the spring of 2013, I was feeling bold and brash. I was thriving in my career, I felt like I had complete control of my life and everything in it, and the world was my oyster. What I really was, was blind. I had been deeply depressed months before and had visited a general practitioner for assistance. As many doctors do, I was simply given a prescription for *benzos* to take for acute relief of symptoms, and was ushered out the door. Although I've never been one to solicit a doctor for drugs, when they prescribe them, I am generally given to abusing them. I felt on top of the world, but I was really just high on Xanax.

The day that my life changed started like any other. I woke up early, picked up a coworker on my 90-minute commute to the office, worked all day, and on the ride home, my friend and I decided we'd indulge in a little vice and visit a strip club. Naturally, alcohol must be consumed in such a place, and consume it we did. By 11 p.m., we were both high on my Xanax, drunk after splitting a case of beer, and ready to call it a night. Getting an Uber was never a thought—I was fine to drive and had done so many times before. I was on top of the world and in complete control, remember?! So drive we did.

We made it back to his place without incident and while there, another friend, his housemate, begged me not to drive any further—to park my car and stay there overnight. I was fine to drive, I had made it this far, after all. I left. I was in control. I could operate the doors, the wheel, and the pedals. I wasn't in control of my judgment.

As I came out of a traffic circle (roundabout, for some), the sheer ecstasy of hitting race lines with the turbo whine in my ear and the driver's seat hurtling me forward as I floored the gas was irresistible. So pleasurable was this ten-seconds in time that I didn't notice I was rapidly approaching a State Trooper squad car at a dead stop in the passing lane waiting to turn left while I was going almost double the speed limit and passing on the right in the slow lane. As soon as I passed them, I realized what I was in for and started to brake before they could turn on their lights to pull me over. I stopped, they arrested me, and I spent the night in jail, still too high and arrogantly indignant to think I was in the wrong for driving in such a state. This was a microcosm of the state of my entire life at the time. I wasn't in a good place, I wasn't happy, I wasn't in control. I covered that up and lied to myself with substance abuse. After I was released from jail, I was at rock bottom.

I was convinced I was going to lose everything—my wife, my children, my home, my job—all of it. I certainly deserved to lose them all, and I probably still do. Like a desperate, drowning man, I found myself grasping for anything that would save me from drowning. In my panic I was pulling everyone down to drown with me. In this state, hours after spending the night and following morning in the county jail, I went to visit my first Alcoholics Anonymous meeting.

Although I didn't recognize it at the time, the first bit of true kindness I experienced came from my wife, my friends, and my parents. They had been showing me love, kindness, and good will all along, but I couldn't see past my own ego well enough to express gratitude. Despite violating the vows of our marriage just hours prior, my wife had a bottomless reserve of fortitude and drove me to, and sat with me through, that first meeting. My mother and a good friend came with me as well, expressing how much they cared about my wellbeing despite how broken an individual I was in that moment.

I was deeply embarrassed and terrified to confront who I really was when I walked through the doors of a church whose denomination I'd never even heard of before. What happened next was absolutely shocking to me. I was welcomed warmly and without an ounce of judgment. I didn't understand how or why at the time, but the people who attend AA for years look at newcomers like me and see their own past selves. They know the desperate depths I had reached, and having been there themselves, they wished such a continued fate on no one. They offered me their hands to pull me from my despair.

I had no idea how to react to such an act of kindness. I was a complete stranger that none of these people had met before. I was a broken man with open wounds and a fractured soul. Despite all this, they shared their own life stories with me and listened to mine without passing judgment. I wept like a child in front of a room full of strangers as I recounted the events from the evening before.

In spite of what I'd told them, without regard to its recency, they gave me encouragement. This group of merciful volunteers, and many others just like them in other AA meetings I went on to attend in the following months, gave me a voice to speak my truth without judgment. They gave me grace and forgiveness I will never deserve.

They encouraged me to live in the present and acknowledge that the past is past and cannot be changed. They encouraged me to keep telling my story at meetings, so even if I was only hours removed from my last drink, I could help the next person stumbling in the door who was drunk. They encouraged me to take it slow, and learn to forgive myself and how to sincerely apologize to others without expectation of acceptance.

Although I never went back to that particular meeting again because of the time and distance, I did begin attending meetings on a regular basis at a variety of other locations. This became very difficult for me to do on my own after my driver's license was taken away (which occurs after the court has processed your case, not at the time of arrest).

Very early in this exploration, I met a fellow alcoholic who we'll call John. John is a physician, and he cared so deeply about giving back that after my license was suspended, he would go out of his way to come to my home, pick me up, take me to a meeting, and drop me back off. John lived over thirty minutes away. This is so great a human, that he would take two hours he could have been spending doing anything he pleased, and he spent them retrieving me and dropping me off, all for my benefit. He was positively delighted to do it and only cared that I was making meetings and staying sober. To this day, this remains one of the most selfless acts I have ever encountered, and I was the beneficiary.

I also found great kindness in the hearts of the people I worked with, both my employer and my customers. I quickly found out after my incident that my immediate supervisor suffered from his own struggles with alcoholism. He went out of his way to make sure the jobs I was working could be done mostly remotely so that a lack of a driver's license wouldn't be majorly impactful. He also shared his stories with me, and listened to my story when I needed it.

Unfortunately, when everything first happened, I was in the middle of a job that required me to commute four hours per day. As a matter of professionalism, I had to communicate to my customer that my ability to come onsite was compromised. The CIO of that organization made it clear to me, and to his account team at my company, that I was to remain engaged on his project and that he would accept no one else. He also created exceptions to policies that would have made it difficult for me to complete the work remotely. To put this in perspective, this individual could have easily demanded another engineer, or potentially even nullified the contract I was executing—a multi-million dollar act of kindness.

It has taken me years to come to terms with who I was, and I'm still not completely certain I have, but those dark times and events and the rebuilding that followed have dramatically altered the course of my life. I hadn't known a life without substance abuse before then. I grew up around it and in it. The kindness given to me by multiple groups of strangers set me on a path to learn how to lead a fulfilling life grounded in reality, and taught me how to confront hardship head-on without cowering from it behind the fog of drunkenness.

It reconnected me with Jesus who I had renounced many years before. It helped me learn that virtuous living can be far more fulfilling than one full of the depravity found at the bottom of a bottle. By design, I know none of the real names of those whom I've shared a meeting with, but I owe them all a debt of gratitude that can never be repaid. With their aid, I have gained strength of will. I honor their service to me by doing all that I can to harness that inner strength in service of others who find themselves at rock bottom.

As a parting aside, if you or someone you know is suffering from addiction, please visit an AA meeting. The only judgment you will find there is that which you pass on yourself. It is also a common misconception that Step 2 (a higher power) must be Jesus. Although it was Jesus for me, all faiths (including no faith in the form of atheism) are welcome. The meetings do end with the "Our Father" Christian prayer, but you're not required to say it, and no one will judge you for abstaining. I can't emphasize enough how much good these groups perform.

Jackson Phillips

The Accidental Shoplifter

Everyone knows what a shoplifter is. It's a teenaged prankster in CVS who stashes five bottles of nail polish in her purse and darts out to show her friends the loot. Or it's a desperate father in Walmart who furtively shoves a pair of sneakers in his backpack so his kid will have something to wear. Well, I am neither of those people, but I was a shoplifter.

One Saturday afternoon in January of 1996, shortly after the holiday season, my fiancé, Larry, and I were strolling through Haddonfield, New Jersey's ritzy shopping district, browsing in the newly quiet boutiques. I shivered under layers of sweaters and a green cloth coat, my breath curling visibly in the cold sunlight. We stopped in Larry's favorite store, Puzzles and Pageantry, admiring the unique toys on display, then we browsed in my favorite store, Thaine's, ogling at their handcrafted curios.

Before circling back to Larry's office, we decided to check out one shop we had never visited before, a small jewelry store nestled off an alley. Gemstones sparkled in its window, drawing me in. The gray-haired shopkeepers welcomed us inside. I inched alongside the glass display cases, eying the diamond pendants and finely wrought filagree earrings within.

"Would you like to look at anything?" the kindly shopkeeper, Mrs. Smith, asked.

"Maybe," I replied, glancing at Larry.

"You should!" Larry said. "What do you like?"

With quiet excitement, I continued to gaze into the glass cases until I saw them: a platinum ring set with a glittering blue topaz, circled with tiny diamonds, and a blue topaz bracelet, its aqua colored gemstones glinting in the cold January sunlight. "May I see these?" I asked.

"Of course," Mrs. Smith smiled.

The ring sparkled on my finger and the bracelet, a circle of pale blue light, hugged my wrist. I felt like a princess, like Cinderella. I had never worn such elegant jewelry before. Larry beamed. Ever since we began to date, he loved to lavish me with gifts.

The store was quiet. No other customers were there. We chatted with Mr. and Mrs. Smith, an older couple who had maintained this jewelry store for thirty years. We talked about working in Haddonfield and about the busy Christmas shopping season that had recently concluded. Meanwhile the cool sun began to descend in the frosty sky. It was time to return to Larry's office. I gave the shopkeepers the shimmering ring and thanked them for their time. Cheerfully Larry and I strolled back to his office.

Once inside Larry's warm office we removed our gloves, coats, and sweaters. There, on my newly exposed arm, I saw it: the glittering blue bracelet! My heart racing, I found the jewelry store's phone number, called, and informed them we have the bracelet. We will hurry back to return it, we assured them

And so we did.

Ten minutes later, we were back at Smith's Jewelers, apologizing profusely. I returned the bracelet, shaking. I could not believe what I had done.

Mrs. Smith explained, calmly, "We knew that you walked out with the bracelet. We weren't worried about it." Looking at Larry, she added, "We know you work in Haddonfield. We could find you."

Grateful for Mrs. Smith's patience I was, nevertheless, horrified by my own carelessness. "I'm so sorry," I continued. "Really. I have never done this before. I'm not that kind of person. It was the coat sleeve. I couldn't see my wrist. I can't believe I did this!"

Mrs. Smith laughed. "I know. We've had this store for thirty years. We know people." Her empathy, her forgiveness, comforted me. Evidently, she trusted me more than I trusted myself. She paused, then added, "You must really like the bracelet."

"I do," I said, sheepishly. "It's beautiful." And it was. The pale blue crystals glinted in the waning daylight that slanted through the store's broad windows.

Larry pulled me aside. "Would you like this bracelet?" he asked.

I was floored. It's so expensive! Larry was not deterred.

Two months later, at our wedding, the blue topaz bracelet glistened on my wrist.

Twenty-six years later, I marvel at Mrs. Smith's patience. I am not capable of such trust, but I am grateful that she was.

Deborah Schizer Scott

The Light in Judith's Eyes

Glastonbury in the English countryside and the Great Pyramids of Egypt were two of the most magical places I've ever traveled to. Though many miles apart and completely antithetical in culture, they both had something in common. Both locations had a very condensed web of Ley lines—veins of positive energy running just beneath the surface of the earth. Without going into the science of it all, it's speculated that when a certain amount of them overlap, it could be the cause for supernatural phenomena to occur on the surface the earth. If one does find themselves caught in the web of one of these highly charged areas, it could possibly intensify whatever experience you're having in that moment. A perfect storm, in a sense. In my case, it was a perfect spiritual storm.

I believe these Ley lines act like a kind of earthly libido, an invisible chemistry that binds nations and people in inexplicable ways. Glastonbury is located in the Northern Hemisphere of Europe and shares continental land masses with Afro-Eurasia, Asia and Africa. Fraught with myths, legends and Ley lines, it's rumored to be the burial place of King Arthur and Lady Guinevere. The cradle of Christianity, it supports monasteries, monks, the myth of The Holy Grail and fairies. As a visitor, these were some of the stories that captured my imagination. And I wasn't the only one.

Local residents don't even question the notion of fairies. As an average American I had an unaverage curiosity for the world of magical things, oracles and the mythology associated with things like the pyramids and the Holy Grail. I wished I'd been privileged to have met one of those tiny fairies in the flesh. I swear I could feel their presence. However, the closest I would get was only to be teased by the possibility.

Egypt, on the other hand, is famous for its temples, mummies and pyramids. The Egyptians were considered an advanced society that practiced divination and believed that the Pharaohs were connected to the pantheon of gods and goddesses of a much larger universe. They had an impressive array of inventions that not only included advanced medicine and technology but the plow, hieroglyphics and toothpaste. All that rich food and wine! I suppose stained teeth were a result of their overindulgences which led them to the clever invention of toothpaste!

But the pyramids! A complete and mysterious phenomenon in and of themselves, scientists still speculate as to whether or not they were built by aliens or slaves. When I first set foot on the desert floor of the Sahara, my legs melted like chocolate in the heat, and I began to cry for what felt like a coming home. I could feel this energy course up through me and pierce my heart with a dramatic sense of familiarity. I had no known ancestry or logical explanation to bind me to this ancient land and yet the connection was indescribably powerful.

How odd, to be so comfortable here, I thought.

I had lived in L.A. my entire life and never had a single moment where I felt this kind of *at-homeness*. I didn't sleep the entire two weeks I was there. I was so excited to be in this foreign, but not so foreign, land and fell in love with the dust on my clothes and the Arabian horses I rode through the Sahara at midnight. I would soon meet Judith, and become acquainted with the vastness of my own soul and my angels.

Timeless antiquity? Ley lines of unpredictable adventure? Or... could this be one of those past life experiences? I was with a metaphysical tour group and heard the murmurs from the other women, various accounts of them being told they were Cleopatra in a past life. I didn't understand how multiple people could be reincarnated as the same person, but just knew I didn't need to compete for the title. I do believe in past life connections, but this seemed like a housewives stretch of the imagination.

I quietly went about my business and found my way into a group preparing to make the climb inside the King's

Tomb. There was going to be an open eye meditation facilitated by an unassuming woman named Judith Larkin. Judith had acquired the humble appearance of a librarian for her exterior self. She was an older woman clad in Bermuda shorts, a white sun hat and conservative sunglasses. Camouflaged in the guise of an average American citizen, Judith had a unique and powerful gift. She had an extraordinary ability to transport one's perceptions into a world beyond by simply gazing into their eyes.

We were instructed on this night inside the tomb to not make any sudden moves while she was in this state, as it could possibly put her in danger and hurt her if we did. She compared it to lying on a table about to have open heart surgery. My friend Craig and I were up for the adventure and quickly found our seats on the cold floor of the tomb, sitting cross-legged with eager anticipation. We did not want to miss this opportunity!

You have to be spiritually open to discover new things and learning to feel energy was a big part of what this trip was about. I'm forever grateful to Craig for inviting me to join him on this spiritual quest. It would change my life forever.

Within minutes of looking into Judith's eyes, I began to see pure energy fields. Patterns of light dancing in front of me. Where there was once a human body, I was now witness to psychedelic, swirling particles of light. My fellow meditators literally disappeared and evaporated into the ethers of where or what I do not know. I started to panic, and as soon as fear crept into my consciousness, it all stopped abruptly. and I was back in the familiar three-dimensional world.

After the meditation, I described my experience to her. She simply said that my meditation was vibrating faster than the speed of light. *Cool!* I thought. Then, I was off to ride some camels around the Great Pyramids at sunset. I was so naïve and caught up in the limitations held inside the pigmentation of my own white skin. I could have just as well been jumping on the merry-go-round at the Santa Monica Pier. I really didn't absorb the implications of what Judith was about to tell me.

"Ellen" she cried, in a soft but eager tone. "Wait! I have something I must reveal to you!" "I don't think you realize it, but you're channeling a lovely stream of angels."

She paused. "You think it's all you, don't you?"

"Huh?" I said. "I had no idea. But I've always felt protected." Then, I quickly ran off into the sunset to rendezvous camels back around the pyramids. Eager to grab all touristy offerings, I didn't look back, nor did I fully take in the depth of what Judith was trying to convey. However, the information and insight she channeled that day changed my life forever. Her heart was so open and pure, she had no reason to single me out except that she felt it was important for me to know a bigger picture. Coming from Los Angeles and being in the film industry I was not used to someone *giving* just because. Whether it was acting or the work I did as a foley artist, there was always something that would exist in the "unspoken" expectation.

The expectation to acquiesce to a director's EGO and artistic demands or some kind of sexual favor. Judith's open heart combined with the special light in her eyes were unrecognizable forms of communication. I had no reference point for this kind of generosity and kindness!

It turns out Judith had her own church of followers back home in San Diego but gave it up because she felt her congregation was confusing their unique experiences with true spiritual growth. This was a greater testimony to her truth as a modern-day prophet and what I interpreted as a soothsayer to my personal journey. A messenger from the beyond, if you will.

I may not have gotten the opportunity to meet the aloof fairies of Glastonbury, but I did get to meet my angels in Egypt. Thank you, Judith, for providing a bridge for me to connect heaven on earth, and thank you to the Ley lines for magnifying the experience so that I might finally listen to a bigger voice. Otherwise, I may have just gone on thinking it was all about me.

Ellen Heuer

Waves of Kindness

Making my home in Honolulu and traveling to the Bay Area regularly for business always was joyful. Getting to the East Bay from the San Francisco airport took many forms—a mini-bus, BART, even a friend's car on occasion. On this particular trip, I needed to go to Berkeley, and I jumped into one of those mini-vans that allowed everyone to pay as we got in, and sometimes when things were busy, we could pay once we were leaving the van.

On this occasion, I struck up a late-night conversation in the van with a very nice fellow who owned his own company, and was a jovial compatriot on this 45-minute drive. We exchanged pleasantries and talked about our families, and by the end of the conversation he knew I had two wonderful girls, and a wife who put up with my many trips to the Mainland.

As we reached the East Bay, he discovered he had lost his wallet, which was much to his everlasting chagrin as he needed to pay the driver. As I am someone who deeply believes in the Aloha spirit (kindness in this case), I offered to pay for him, and he accepted. He ended our conversation as he departed the van with a promise that his company would send me something in the mail.

Well, I didn't count on anything, but thought that one more person on the Mainland would know about the Aloha spirit. This was all I needed to know. Several months later, however, two packages arrived in the mail, and both were good-sized packages. I opened them with pleasant anticipation as Lyn, my wife, and I had not ordered anything (this was pre-Amazon). Each package contained a kit for making a beautiful skateboard, and as I thought back to my conversation with this fine man, he had mentioned that the company he owned was a skateboard company.

Again, an example of the Aloha spirit, or kindness. Needless to say, my two daughters were ecstatic. Having had this wonderful experience, I was able to communicate this level of kindness to my daughters. The Aloha Spirit, and most specifically kindness, has been a part of our lives, especially since the lovely skateboards arrived.

Carl Ackerman

Communities of Kindness

When acts of kindness are performed, we often think of family, friends, or a perfect stranger that is available for someone else's need of encouragement. Kindness can also be expressed when saying or doing something that is totally unexpected to put a smile on the recipient's face.

Society tends to associate acts of kindness with family and friends, though, which can be far from the truth. I grew up in a non-supportive household of strict discipline and constant criticism along with little association with others. The concept of *random acts of kindness* was non-existent to me. I was afraid to reach out and express my inner self. Although a straight "A" student, I was often belittled and cursed at to the point I believed there was no hope due to the shame that was developing within my inner being.

This sense of shame lasted until around age 50. At that point, I joined several community organizations. I was amazed to find that there were supportive individuals that threw compliments my way. It took several years before I could process other people's genuine acts of kindness. Compliments from, "way to go," "you rock," when moderating a committee, to "I wish everyone could be as committed as you are," when serving as an area director were pivotal points for me to turn the many years of shame around into a better self-image.

I remember heading up the Stewardship Committee at my church. Our theme was to "go whole hog" and host a pig roast. Everyone on the committee was supportive, which built my self-esteem. I received all positive remarks such as "You're doing a great job,"; "Way to go, Rich," and "We could never do this without you," as acts of kindness. These statements were meant from the heart and made me feel accepted in their presence. When I got up to the pulpit to provide a quick *Stewardship Thought of the Day*, compliments such as, "...sounds like you came from Harvard University," and, "You have the voice of a sports announcer" were also random acts of kindness as I connected to them as being genuine.

For many years, I felt lonely and felt removed from the world. I woke up every day with a fast pulse and a sense of dread. I was afraid to reach out to anyone to share my concerns. Then the phone rang. On the other end was the senior pastor who asked me how I was doing and offered to bring over fresh fruit and vegetables. He assured me that everything would be okay. All of a sudden, I went from a sense of dread to a sense of reassurance and comfort.

As an offshoot of the church, I was also a member of their singing group. We sang at assisted living facilities, nursing homes and rotary clubs. To my surprise, there was a fabulous cook in our group that would invite everyone over for an annual holiday party. She prepared an entire buffet of homemade appetizers, casseroles and desserts. Her husband also made the best bloody Mary shots ever! I had no idea of this annual party until becoming a member of this group, and receiving a formal invite. I was overcome with both joy and gratitude.

Members of my Toastmasters International organization have been very supportive in my journey to become a better public speaker and leader. My speech evaluators continue to provide constructive feedback for areas to work on for my improvement. I take their feedback as acts of kindness with the underlying intention to promote my self-development.

People of every age and ethnic background need assurance and reassurance that everything will be okay. A pat on the back, a compliment, a hug or a positive vibe can all be construed as acts of kindness.

The corporate world also provided random acts of kindness for me. When my boss told me things such as, "Great job," "Please do not retire too soon," or, "…wished I could have given you a larger raise," all of these comments had a clear message that elevated my status.

I was completely caught off guard some time ago when named Employee of the Month. Although I headed up several internal committees and provided leadership to numerous members, the last thing I was expecting was for management to recognize me in this way. I humbly accepted the award and regarded this as a genuine and random act of kindness.

I will always remember my 25th anniversary with my company. They flew me across the country for a dinner celebration and an overnight stay in San Francisco. We had a nice dinner with presents at each table, a great room to stay in, and a wonderful buffet breakfast before departing the following morning. I walked up and down the steep narrow roads, visited the trolley car museum and Fisherman's Wharf, and saw the Golden Gate Bridge. I felt honored to be recognized for my years of service, and certainly believed this to be a random act of kindness.

From my perspective, in many instances, the family environment, friends, and others you believe in may not provide the acts of kindness needed to instill you with a sense of love, security and self-worth. I propose for everyone to gain perspective from a nonbiased third party that will not be judgmental. Joining community organizations and seeking supportive places of employment are viable steps in the right direction to bring us to a better sense of wholeness. Church, Toastmasters International and my place of employment have continued to provide me with an abundance of personal development, which helps to make a difference in my daily life. If we all were so fortunate, I think the world would be a better place for everyone.

Given my experiences, acts of kindness from outside organizations did in fact end up changing and shaping my life and inner being. Although family was not my supportive entity, acts of kindness via community service have played a big role in shaping my positive perspective and inspiring me to become a better person.

Richard Kouhoupt

The Vaccine Angel's Wings Ring True

I was a Covid bride. Widowed at age 47 in 2012. After nearly eight years on my own, Mark, also a widow, and I reconnected. Mark and I got engaged on March 9th, 2020. We decided to marry a year later. Within two weeks, the country began to shut down. We didn't expect it to last more than a few weeks, so we continued to plan. It couldn't last a year, could it?

A hall, a caterer, a wedding gown and bridesmaid dresses finalized as we approached the summer surge. We were certain that by fall we would all be safe. We saw a brief reprieve. In August, we were able to do a small outdoor socially-distanced family gathering to celebrate. Shortly after, we did the same, albeit separately with the bridal party.

Given we thought we would never marry again, we planned a wedding for 200 people. We're old, with quite a few people from the families of two very successful marriages plus many friends who we wanted to celebrate with. Invitations and party favors ordered in bulk. As an over-planner, I was in my element. A website was established. A photographer and DJ along with other vendors were contracted with deposits.

Then the second surge hit. Our guest list slowly tumbled from 200 to 150 to 90 down to 25. Keeping in touch with vendors on a regular basis, we could have rescheduled or simply married quietly, but the wedding was to be a celebration uniting our families. We weighed the pros and cons of postponing it. In talking to most vendors, we would be scheduling in late 2022 or even 2023. We trudged forward, deciding that we would marry even if we just had our children and close friends there. I diligently watched every Covid briefing, working to understand and adjust plans to ensure we had everything covered.

We ordered red, yellow and green bracelets for people who, respectively, wanted to be left alone, were okay talking and okay touching. We packed individual favor boxes to be set on tables to avoid having community favor tables. We bought a case of sanitizer to place around the room in addition to the sanitizer favors. We had boxes of paper masks, bridal party masks that matched their clothing and his-and-her bride and groom masks. Ultimately, we decided to have a Mardi Gras theme which allowed us to give some air cover to the masks in the photos as we bought individual glittered and colored masks for each guest to brighten the mood.

We had contingency plans for contingency plans in case Covid interfered. For example, we not only had a wedding officiant, but had a backup officiant from the bridal party, and my daughter as their backup. We found someone to do an online webcast of our wedding so guests could attend long distance.

Our videographer/photographer informed us the week of the wedding that they were not able to make it that week, so he found another company and also worked with the person doing the online webcast of our wedding to take enough footage to turn our beautiful ceremony into memories on video and photos. During planning, the reception rules continued to change so we went from reception, to champagne toast, only to snacks on the way out, back to a toast and finally a few days before, the wedding restrictions were eased so we were able to go back to a sit-down dinner as long as we were done by 10 p.m. We were not allowed to have dancing among guests, so we focused on how to make it entertaining by remaining socially distant.

During wedding planning, Mark and I had scheduled our first vaccine shot for two weeks before the wedding with the second due a week after, which coincidentally fell on my birthday. We timed it so we were past the side effects by the week of the ceremony. We went to a mass vaccine distribution center at 8 a.m. We were in and out quickly.

However, while waiting fifteen minutes after our shot for any side effects to subside, I noticed a woman wearing angel wings and a halo, a Valentine holiday vest and a big smile walking around the waiting area of the mega center. Her job was to sanitize the seats after each person left the waiting area. She would dance to the music playing on the speakers, and would smile and joke around with people. Her personality and costume made an impression on me.

The week of the wedding, we encountered more ups and downs. With four days to go, we were finally given the count of 65 guests, so we spent two days talking to folks and narrowing it down to the final list, adding and removing family as final decisions were made by family members now wary of attending on their end. Everyone was wonderful.

A few days after the wedding, we were scheduled for our second vaccine. I decided to prepare Mark a home-cooked meal. My friends are chuckling now, knowing how much I love *not* to cook. I found a recipe for stew and proceeded to add the ingredients. My new husband loved it but let's just say it didn't love him. The volume of sodium in the stew triggered vertigo that was bad enough to send him to the hospital the night before we were to have our second vaccine. Which also happened to be just two days before Mark and I were planning to take a long-awaited trip to the Grand Canyon where we could quarantine and recover from the wedding planning of the prior few months.

He went in through the Emergency Room with all of its buzzers, beeps and bells. They did all the things they do in the Emergency Room. Once they determined he couldn't go home, they found him a room and told me to reschedule his second vaccine for the following Monday, which was five days after the original schedule and our original planned date of arrival at the Grand Canyon. I started replanning the trip to the Grand Canyon. Flights without change fees during Covid? Who knew.

Mark and I decided I would still get vaccinated. No sense in either of us being exposed any longer than necessary. I would leave Mark at the hospital, go home that night, then get up in the morning for my second dose.

The alarm went off. I got out of bed. Let the dogs out and grabbed coffee. I'm not sure if I brushed my teeth or not. The combination of the months of planning and replanning the wedding, the anticipation of the vaccine and Mark in the hospital led to my emotional cup filled all the way to the brim. I had an 8 a.m. appointment at the mass distribution center. I wanted to get in and out so I could go see Mark and find out when he would be released.

I got there as they were opening. It was the same as the first time: no issues getting in or through the shot line. As I went to sit in the waiting area, I once again saw the 100 or so seats lined up in rows of 10 by 10, all six feet apart. This time, the angel lady with her magic spray bottle was wiping seats in the row next to mine. She was dressed in green, with green tinsel hair and a shamrock sweater. She was an ebullient leprechaun bopping around to Michael Jackson's *Billy Jean* as she cleaned. Her smile and zest for life was similar to that on our last encounter.

Watching her, my vaccine record card fell from my hand and she bent to pick it up. She noticed the date below my name. She whispered to me, "It's your birthday" and I must have looked surprised. But it *was*. With everything swirling around me, I had forgotten that it was my birthday!

Her next words were "We're going to sing to you," and she proceeded to lead those around me in a brief round of *Happy Birthday* that had half the room singing by the time it was done. They didn't know my name so they all sort of mumbled that part. At that moment, however, I thought about how many people must have walked through that center. How many people were apprehensive? How many people were Covid-fatigued? How many people did she bring a smile to their face like she did mine?

My story isn't so much about the zany wedding preparations that occurred during the Covid pandemic, but more about the reactions and life-affirming echo that is created by someone just being kind in daily life. At a moment like that, the ringing of birthday bells was magnified during these times by a chance crossing of paths when I most needed it. I will forever remember her kind spirit and how she made me feel.

Donna McCart Welser

Making His House My Home

Kindness comes in all shapes and sizes. It comes in the form of smiles, waves, hugs, personalized gifts, surprise parties, anonymous donations, moments of paying it forward, tributes, and so much more. I was raised to give of myself to others who need help, a kind shoulder, an ear to listen and a safe space to share. I applaud my parents and extended family for teaching me these tools. I can safely say I am a good friend, a reliable worker, and I embrace everyone.

What I do not do well is accept acts of kindness. I know this sounds funny, but honestly, I would rather give than receive. I would rather remain anonymous than be praised. I'd rather use my skills for good without recognition than be honored for just doing what I feel is the right thing to do. So, when I am the recipient of an act of kindness, it's overwhelming to me. I appreciate it and I am thankful for it, but...

When I first moved to Wolfville in the Fall of 2002, I knew the town because of my time at Acadia University but I didn't know how I would find my place in the community. I was fortunate to live in the basement apartment of then-Mayor Bob Stead and his partner Danny, who not only gave me a place to live but also saw something in me that made them want to include me in their house gatherings, garden parties, and town outings. Prior to then, I had never met Bob or Danny, but they had heard I was looking for a place. I had some references through my job at the time and everything fell into place.

With Bob being mayor, as well as a prominent community member and an advocate for the LGBTQ+ community, I was introduced to the many wonderful movers and shakers of our community and Bob made sure I was welcomed and heard, and that there was a place for me.

Bob would introduce me with "This is Mike Butler, and one day, he's going to run the town", and after my heart returned to its regular beat, I carried on with whatever conversation I was having. I shook many hands, I attended many meetings in his garden about how to improve our community, and I spoke with Bob many times following meetings, as he saw me as a young, vibrant member of Wolfville who had concerns and a voice. For the 14 years I lived in that quaint little apartment, Bob treated me with so much respect. Having a man in a prominent position in municipal politics care about my thoughts, my safety, and my future meant more to me than I can ever put into words.

Bob was a quiet fighter who had lived through so many eras of the gay rights movement. He was part of so much change that would directly affect myself and many of my generation of LGBTQ+. And in doing that, he inspired us to do the same for others. There is an expression within the community that says to "gay it forward", which means to create a safe space, do a good deed within the community and always be there for the good and the bad.

I didn't realize it at the time, but Bob was preparing me in many ways for when the time came that I wanted to be part of municipal politics. I was young, but he saw something in me that clearly pointed to a greater contribution to my town and its residents. He trusted my opinion, saw how well I interacted with people, applauded my volunteerism, my connectivity to the community and he always commented how proud he was of me for my work ethic and determination to make the town better, especially for those in the Queer community.

Bob Stead became my friend, above all else. He served our town and its residents with the utmost care and consideration. He and I shared many glasses of wine, many Wolfville and life-related chats, and for 14 and a half years, he shared his home with me. His house was a safe space for everyone, and my basement apartment was where I created a safe space for others.

Bob passed away in 2014, but he is never far from my mind. A while after his passing, I moved into a new apartment with my boyfriend. In July 2018, he and I became the first same-sex marriage to be held at the chapel at Acadia University. Each year, a Pride Flag is raised in Wolfville to commemorate Pride Month and the International Day Against Homophobia and Transphobia, traditions Bob had started. I know, and will argue forever, that I would not be who I am and not be what I am to the community without Bob.

In the Fall of 2020, I ran for a position on the Wolfville Town Council and won one of the six seats; I even earned the most votes! Now, I can help others. I am now able to assist with bylaws, planning and development of the town, implementing ideas that will make positive changes. Without Bob's kindness and generosity, who knows what might have happened?

Mike Butler

When You Gotta Go

I used to do my banking at University Credit Union. Whenever I went, no matter the time of day, there would be a long line of people waiting for their moment with the teller. But I liked going there. They didn't charge a monthly fee. Another plus: they charged very little for a bounced check. (Not that I ever bounce a check.)

I was often in a rush to make a deposit, use the ATM or do whatever I had to do. For some odd reason, almost every time I went to UCU, I needed to pee. The few times I did use their bathroom, it disturbed my delicate sensibilities with its grubby walls and stale air—like it hadn't been cleaned in days. It also looked as if the tile floor was coated with a layer of grime. After roughing it a few times, I avoided using the bathroom whenever possible—unless I reached the point of desperation.

One hot miserable day in July, 2015, I once again found myself in a long line waiting for a teller. At the very front was a young woman in an African yellow and black print dress and matching head wrap. An adorable little boy of a year or so was perched on her hip. The baby was jabbering up a storm, providing the weary customers with a sweet distraction as we awaited our turn. Next in line was a sweaty 20-something guy in workout clothes, who—to tell the truth—had a lot of nerve coming into a place of business dressed like that. The man right behind him was keeping his distance (for obvious reasons) and so on and so on until the line reached the woman standing in front of me.

She wore a navy business suit and crisp white blouse (impressive on a sweltering day). She looked to be in her mid-60s, with Hershey skin, full beautiful lips in crimson red, hair in dreads and an approachable air.

"You know," I said, moving a step closer to her, "I always seem to come here when there is a long line. I wish they had more tellers."

"I know what you mean," she said in a soft voice. "The same thing happens to me." She made a full turn and smiled at me.

"My problem," I confided, "is while I'm waiting, I always need to go to the bathroom." She nodded in sympathy—always so validating from a stranger.

"Because of these long lines," I continued, "I have to hold it until I practically burst." Why I am telling her all of this, I cannot explain to you. She waved her finger at me.

"**Girl,**" she said, "her voice maternal and knowing "you gotta go when you gotta go. You should not hold it in. That is **not healthy!**" We smiled at each other in sisterhood.

"Thank you," I said. "That is good advice."

Seven years later, when I am out somewhere and wonder if I should find a bathroom or hold it, I hear her voice in my head:

"Girl, that is not healthy!"

Although our time together was just a few minutes, and I'm not sure I would recognize her if I saw her again, this woman—whose name I do not know—and her wise advice has stayed with me all these years. I remember her with the kind of joy that comes with unexpected connections. When I tell this story (which I have many times since that day) it always warms my heart. I wish I could thank her once again, to let her know how she changed my life for the better.

Linda Goldman

ACT Five

A runner saw a competitor
injured, in quite a bind
She stopped to finish the race with her
which pushed her far behind
"But you trained so hard to win that race"
some critics lost their mind
The rest of us knew she really won
by being just that kind.

Matthew J. Goldberg

The Dad and the Dude

I'm on the way home to New Jersey from Washington, DC, driving my old, beat-up car on I-95 North. Nobody else is in my car. If memory serves, I'm driving a rusted-out 1970 Oldsmobile Cutlass that once was a sharp maroon. That was before I owned it and further hastened its decline. I'm in my early 20s, and one might accurately describe me as young, book smart and *street-dumb*. Literally and figuratively street-dumb.

It's the 1980s, and it's an era before I started belonging to a road service club, and long before anyone started using a cell phone. As a newer, street-dumb driver, I don't immediately recognize that sudden, thumping sound from the right rear of my car. In short order, though, even I realize what's up. *Oh man, a flat tire*, I exclaim. To nobody else.

I maneuver safely to the right shoulder, dodging that initial hazard. Now, I had finally learned how to change a tire shortly before the sudden flat, but I never had to do it in an emergency. I could only do it in optimal conditions from my driveway.

In the light drizzle, I search my trunk, and find softball equipment, a basketball and some fast-food wrappers. Well, that was helpful. A further search—no doubt without a flashlight…as if I'd ever need one—reveals a spare tire. But no jack.

No problem, as I remembered just having passed a big service station. I lock up my car, and start to walk what I presumed would be, at most, a five-minute stroll. But 15 minutes later, there's not a gas station in sight, and the heavens have erupted. That refreshing light drizzle is now a torrential downpour. I concede defeat and start the rain-drenched footslog back to my Cutlass. Certainly, I will come up with a Plan B once inside my car.

About five minutes later, a black van pulls up beside me, and the front passenger rolls down his window. I cannot remember their names, so I will accord myself some poetic license and dub them *The Dad and the Dude.*

The Dude speaks first. "Hey man, can you use a hand? Are you alright?"

Ever *quick* on the uptake, I reply, "I'm okay. But isn't there a gas station around here?"

From the driver's side, The Dad yells at his son. "Dude, tell him to get in the van. He's absolutely soaked."

Both of their faces look friendly enough. Then again, not every friendly face means…ah, never mind, I had barely a trace of distrust or cynicism back then.

I climb into the back of the van, grateful for whatever length of respite I'll have from the Maryland monsoon.

The Dad seems concerned. "You look like you can use some help. What do you need?"

Not so quick on my feet, I reply. "Thanks, guys. I was walking to the gas station. There is one nearby, right?"

The Dude laughs, but in a sympathetic way. "Yeah, I think we passed one about five miles ago."

"Oh, man" I manage.

The Dad asks me why I want to go to a gas station. I tell him about my flat tire.

"Do you have a spare tire and a jack?"

"I have a spare tire and a 33-ounce Louisville Slugger."

(Please note that the Louisville Slugger was mentioned in an innocent, avid-softball-league-player kind of way, so no threat was intended or received.)

"The spare tire will work. We've got a jack in our trunk."

A couple minutes later, they pull behind my car. I step out and grab my spare tire. Who said I wasn't good in a pinch? And then, perhaps out of an extra degree of kindness or probably realizing that I would be no help whatsoever changing the tire, The Dad gives me a generous offer.

"Why don't you sit in my van? It won't take us long to change this. Right, Dude?"

"Yep."

I heed their advice, and I picture myself being almost as useless as young Ralphie *helping* the old man fix his flat tire in "A Christmas Story". (At least, I didn't drop an f-bomb, and later have to wash my mouth out with a bar of Lifebuoy soap. Great movie … but I digress.)

I feel just a little guilty that they're fixing my flat tire in the deluge while I get to hang out in their cool van.

These guys are efficient. I won't say they resemble a pit crew at the Daytona 500, but even if I had a jack and a more mechanically adept passenger with me, it would have taken us at least three times as long as it took them. And they don't even need my Louisville Slugger.

The Dad, ever the leader, gives me the good news. "Your spare still looks pretty good. You should be ready to roll now."

"How can I thank you guys?" I start to go through my near-empty wallet, looking for some way to repay them. "Sorry, I don't have any…"

The Dad, probably embarrassed that I wanted to tip him, has a better solution. "You can do us a favor."

"Yeah, sure."

"Start up your car, and make sure it's okay."

"Sure."

"And one more thing. Try to help someone else out one day. Take it easy, man."

I didn't yet know the expression *Pay it Forward*, but here it was in action. The Cutlass starts right up, they give me a thumbs-up, and the black van is on its way. The rest of my ride home is uneventful, but I wonder what other adventures The Dad and the Dude will encounter. Who else will they save?

All these years later, I have tried to be a kind, caring soul in all situations, but alas, when it comes to emergency car repairs, I am hopelessly street-dumb. Oh, I once sat in my car behind a woman while she called and waited for AAA. But a jack in my hand still isn't any more useful than a Louisville Slugger and a fast-food wrapper.

Matthew J. Goldberg

This Too, Shall Pass

I f you grew up in the United States during the 1980s, like I did, you'd remember the War on Drugs, "Just Say No," and a nightly news diet chronicling random (and some not-so-random) acts of violence perpetrated by drug gangs. The television show *Miami Vice* grabbed top ratings every week as it simultaneously glamorized the lifestyles of vice cops and the drug runners they pursued.

While I lived in relative safety, tucked away in a semi-rural suburb, the culture of drugs and violence was never further than a press of the television "on" button. Or even more conveniently—a press of the "play" button on my knock-off Walkman or comically large boom box.

So it was with amusement that I would read a poster tacked to the wall of the tiny, seventh-grade classroom of one of my teachers, *Ms. H*. It commanded simply, "Practice random acts of *kindness*." Ms. H ran a class for a certain type of special education student. These were kids for, whatever reason, the school powers-that-be determined should receive more intellectually rigorous instruction than the *gen pop* student body. Somehow, I had been classified as one of those students.

I use the term *gen pop* advisedly, as most of the time, school did feel like a prison. The lines, the regimentation, the mess hall-like cafeteria—it all felt like a system designed to train and contain rather than meaningfully educate. Ms. H's class provided a welcome respite, where we learned to think critically and challenge ourselves intellectually. We read tough material, such as *Night*, a memoir by Holocaust survivor Elie Wiesel. Ms. H was something of a rebel and survivor herself, for that time—an out and open lesbian in a conservative, Reagan-worshipping school district. In a place and time and environment where conformity ruled, she stood out for challenging the status quo.

Another placard in her classroom that stuck with me read: "Minds are like parachutes—they only function when open."

***

As with countless other school-age children since there were schools, bullies had posed a problem for me throughout the years. In seventh grade, the particular threat was school bus bullies—they would threaten, harass, and insult, but fortunately had not laid hands on me ... yet. But it was just a matter of time, I knew, before their larger fists would find their way to my vulnerable skull. One day, I decided I'd had enough—in my pre-adolescent, heck, prepubescent mind—a *show of force* seemed like just the solution. No one had to get hurt, but I figured merely flashing a deadly weapon would convince any would-be tormenters that I wasn't worth the effort.

To my way of thinking, it was just like what countries do: "Hey, I might be small, but I have nukes, so don't mess with me" … only on a much smaller scale. This is how pre-teen logic works.

(Fortunately) I didn't have access to nukes, or even a small-caliber handgun. But I did own a mean-looking hunting knife with a six-inch blade. This wasn't some cheap, re-purposed kitchen utensil, mind you. It was intended for gutting and dressing wild game, and it even sported a hollow handle packed with survival gear—matches, plastic rain shelter, fishing line and hooks. I had bought it, with the help of an adult, with my own money after seeing Sly Stallone wield a similar blade in the *Rambo* movies. To say I loved that knife would be a gross understatement.

Long story short, I brought the knife to school one day, stuffing it into my blue Wilson gym bag. I had no intention of using it on anyone—I'd only give my bully a glimpse of it if he started acting a fool again on the bus. The myriad ways this plan could go south hadn't even occurred to my young brain.

I went through the sweltering spring day with an unusual pep in my step—homeroom, social studies, algebra, gym, lunch … As I daydreamed through history class, sometime around 1:30 p.m., one of the gym teachers—

a former college hoops star named "Lefty" Driscoll—pulled me from class and into the hall.

"Akweli," he asked, with a concerned look, "is this your bag?"

He held up a familiar-looking blue duffel bag. For half a second, I considered denying ownership. But I'd seen enough *Columbo* episodes to know I wasn't going to dissemble my way out of this one. I broke out into a flop sweat as I mentally pieced together how he must have tracked me down: In my haste, I'd forgotten the bag—scary knife and all—in the locker room after gym; someone found the knife, along with some incriminating homework assignment with my name on it. Busted.

While this took place well before the era of school shootings and "zero-tolerance" policies, I just knew my life was over. *Now* my mind was properly functioning in *Consequences* mode: Getting caught with a knife would equal expulsion from school. Expulsion would equal a mark on my "permanent record," barring me from college. No college education would equal poverty and homelessness as soon as I reached adulthood.

Okay, so perhaps those extreme conclusions were somewhat overly catastrophizing. But such are the thought patterns of the pre-teen brain. The expulsion part, at least, probably wasn't far off the mark.

"Come with me to Mr. Robison's office, and he'll decide what happens next," Lefty said.

Mr. Robison, the vice principal, served as the school's judge and disciplinarian for the most unruly and disruptive students. A trip to his office meant you were in deep doodoo—a multi-day suspension from class was typically regarded as an excellent outcome.

As I waited outside Robison's office for what felt like an eternity, I contemplated the "ruins" of my barely begun life. Already, suicidal thoughts were creeping in. How would I do it, I wondered? I knew a guy from my karate school who had killed himself at 12 or 13 years old, just a couple years earlier. Good-looking kid, smart, with tons of potential. It puzzled me at the time, but now, frighteningly, *I got it*. I understood the sense of utter hopelessness, however misguided it actually was. Going out on my own terms would restore some sense of *control*, however fleeting.

A parade of teachers, acquaintances, and friends filed by me in the hall, as I sat awaiting Robison. Some of the teachers shot disapproving or quizzical glances—even pre-social media, the news had by now made the rounds of the teachers' lounge many times over: *He was a good kid—why'd he do something like that? Who was he after? Was anyone hurt?*

Eventually, Ms. H strolled by. There was no need to recount the story. Her lips parted in a weary, knowing smile. "You made a mistake," she said, reading my worried face. "I know it seems like the world is ending, but just know that *this, too, shall pass.*"

She patted my shoulder reassuringly, leaving me to ponder those words: "This too, shall pass." (Only much, much later would I learn that it is an ancient Persian adage—perhaps my not knowing its origin lent the phrase even more gravitas and mystical wisdom.)

I tried to think of Elie Wiesel and all he endured—and how my tribulations (this was just the latest in a series of disciplinary gaffes I'd committed that year) paled by comparison.

It was starting to work. I wanted to get through this, to the other side. Even if it meant months of hell in assorted parental and school-administered punishments.

While other teachers clucked their disapproval and gossiped behind the teachers' lounge walls, Ms. H provided the right words, right when I needed them. Her act of empathy quite possibly saved me from committing the ultimate self-harm, and her words now echo in my mind any time circumstance brings major challenges to my life.

It may have seemed like a small kindness to Ms. H, but for me it was a life-altering one. I'd like to think that because of her, I learned to be a more considerate, tolerant, and open-minded human being—one committed to perpetrating random (and perhaps some not-so-random) acts of kindness.

Epilogue

After some strenuous parent-vice principal conferences and a robust repertoire of home and in-school sentencing, I managed to evade expulsion. I made it to university on an academic scholarship, graduated, and became a relatively productive member of society. It easily could have gone in a different direction—if not for the intervention of many caring adults. It just goes to show, you never know when even a small act on your part might change a person's life.

Akweli Parker

Vanity and Humanity

When I was young and vacant, 18 years old and newly married, we moved to Los Angeles, and met my husband's cousins. They were, in my eyes, the epitome of 1960s Hollywood glamour: a beautiful grandmother, Rose, her exquisite daughter Lana, Lana's handsome husband Morry, and their daughters, Arlene, 16, and Tina, 3. Lana was then in her forties, dazzlingly perfect...her house was something out of a *Home Beautiful* magazine, and her face—full lips, and a long straight nose, like a Greek statue. It gave her an imperious look. Her long lashes swept her cheeks, and framed her green eyes. She had platinum blonde hair, a la Marilyn Monroe.

Lana's mother had the button-nosed style of the day, courtesy of Doctor Parks, the popular Beverly Hills plastic surgeon, who later gave Lana's daughters cute, turned-up noses, just like their grandmother.

I realize now that how I thought of Lana over the years reflected my own growth and maturity. At first, I was awed, stunned by her beauty. I found out later that she spent at least three hours at her kitchen table with magnifying mirrors, applying those long eyelashes one by one, adding color to her already perfect skin, lining those eyes, a la Elizabeth Taylor. She was a perfect trophy blond for her handsome, gregarious husband, Morry, who was a top sales executive. His clients were movie stars and she impressed them.

I had a front-row seat to their lives. At first, I was bedazzled and later, horrified, at the amount of time and money she spent to look the way she looked.

I even became kind of disgusted when she told me she had trained herself to sleep on her back without moving, so that she would not ruin her makeup, and would wake up looking beautiful every morning. Her husband almost never saw her without makeup. She never wanted him to see her without makeup and since makeup took so long to apply, she only did it every few days.

I think of her more kindly now, as an artist. She was her own canvas, and that makeup was her palette. She recreated herself over and over, although it was always her perfect young self.

When Lana was in her late 50s, she was diagnosed with ovarian cancer. She had treatment. She became thin, and bald, but she wore beautiful turbans and wigs, and with that perfect face continued to look magnificent, but she was dying.

She decided before she died that she would die in the hospital. She didn't want her family watching her die, and thought they would never feel the same about their home if she died there. She demanded that she not have visitors, not even her husband and daughters. She did not want them, or anyone else, to see her looking bad. They listened to her, and did not go.

I couldn't stand the thought of her lying alone in her hospital bed. I decided to disregard her wishes and go to the hospital.

When I entered her room, I saw a scene I will never forget as long as I live. It was like entering a hushed cathedral, and seeing Michelangelo's Pieta. Lana, now shrunken and tiny, and without a wig, was sitting in the lap of a large black woman, who was holding her.

The contrast was stark. Lana was by then tiny, frail and bald, like a child, her head and her pale face nestled in the breasts of this stranger (*a new nurse or caregiver?*), who was gently rocking her. It was a scene full of pure love. The love was palpable. There was no more vanity. Lana was being seen, stripped naked of all her masks, and loved unconditionally.

The room was peaceful and hushed. I quietly backed out.

I never exchanged a word with either of them, but I still think of that angel of mercy who had the compassion and kindness to cradle Lana in her soft, pillowy arms as if she were a small child and could, by that act, make her know for sure that she was loved, no matter how she looked.

Rachelle Elias

An Angel in the City

I t was a callback! My first musical at New York University in New York City! I had just left a fancy, overpriced singing coach and was heading to the subway to see the much anticipated final cast list of our school's much anticipated musical, *Mame.*

I was 19, maybe 20, singing my heart out to Gershwin and Sondheim all the way to the Red Line at 17th Street.

Hooray, I thought! The subway train goes right down to school. I couldn't wait. Almost on the subway platform, I thought to myself looking around, *"Wait a minute, I think this is an exit, not an entrance. Ahhh, I need to go up to 23rd Street or down to 14th Street."*

As I turned around with all my musical song books stacked against me, ready to bound up the steps, I heard a sound I will never forget: the cock of a gun. I felt it as he pointed it right at my temple. There was a tall, terrifying man looming over me with his friend lurking in the corner to make sure the coast was clear.

Somehow, I knew I was in grave danger and that this man would not hesitate to pull the trigger. What had I done wrong? I was now completely out of my body. I felt like I was in a movie, or an episode of *Law and Order*!

I didn't even hear him ask for my wallet. I just swung my knapsack around from my shoulder, took out my wallet and said, "Hello sir, I have $22, my NYU ID, my Maryland driver's license and a note from my mom." "Here", I said taking the money from the wallet, putting the wallet back in my knapsack and swinging it over my shoulder, all the while the gun still pointed at my head. Once they had the money, they quickly darted up the steps and ran away.

I don't remember how long I was down on the subway platform or much of anything, before I saw an older gentleman with warm eyes and a comforting smile exiting the train. He was wearing a lovely cardigan and a smart looking winter cap and using his cane, I'm sure, for a fashion statement.

Coming back into my body, I found myself running up to him.

"Hello sir, I am up for a musical at school and I just got held up at gunpoint! What direction are you walking in? Could I maybe walk with you for a bit?"

"Of course", he said. "Where are you going, young lady? Let me walk with YOU. Especially on this chilly, snowy day. I'm so sorry that happened to you. You are a very brave girl."

This most beautiful soul locked elbows with mine and we walked and talked more than 30 New York City blocks in the snow down to 721 Broadway—to NYU's main theater building.

As he safely accompanied me in the elevator, I remember him excitedly saying, "Let's see how we did?! I bet we got cast!"

Something about his warmth and compassion for a complete stranger finally released the tears down my face as I realized I was safe.

He gave me his handkerchief to wipe away my tears and fears and said, "I've got a good feeling about this", gesturing to my classmates who suddenly erupted into applause. I was beyond excited and couldn't stop crying, but now they were tears of joy and gratitude.

Just to make sure I got the part, I went to check the cast list and when I turned around to confirm the great news... he was gone.

He was like an angel, a New York City guardian angel. The simple benevolence shown to me that day was humanity at its very best.

Lori Alan

Swinging Sammy

Junior high school (now known as "middle school", although the former only included seventh and eighth grades) is a difficult place for most adolescents. At this age, even the most socially confident youngsters have doubts about their looks and their place in the school's pecking order. Imagine how much more so this would have been for a short, skinny young man with glasses known for his math prowess and love of singing. That young man was me...

In the fall of 1960, I was a student at Jonas E. Salk Junior High in Levittown, New York. The smart alecks among us referred to our school as "Join us and sulk". I found my place there among fellow math geeks and other academic high achievers in general. In eighth grade, I was encouraged by some of these well-meaning friends to run for treasurer of my class. It was felt that my training having worked in my father's sporting goods store for several years made me a likely candidate.

Unfortunately, just before the elections I developed a stye and needed to wear an eye patch during my waking hours. In my carefully crafted speech, I referred to my long experience helping my father make bank deposits and balance accounts at his store. However, because of my patch, I was interrupted by pirate-like "aarrgh" calls many times. Needless to say, I lost the election by a McGovernesque margin. Although my friends who ran for president and vice-president were victorious, I had a difficult time celebrating at the party which followed to congratulate the winners.

My favorite period of the school day was chorus. Our teacher was a man about fifty years old with a bald pate and a ring of graying hair around the lower part of his head. His name was Mr. Samuel Gurstelle and our private nickname for him was "Swinging Sammy". As a high school math teacher for more than forty years, I can only thank those who either volunteered or were forced to teach middle schoolers.

One of my colleagues has referred to students at that age as "hormones with legs", a very apt expression from my experience.

But back to chorus… My voice had not yet changed, and I was seated in the soprano section; couldn't Swinging Sammy at least have let me sing alto?

Determined to enjoy the experience no matter which part I was assigned, I would sing out enthusiastically. I also had a louder voice than most of my soprano cohort, many of whom did not want to attract more attention that necessary to their vocal shortcomings. One day, however, a young lady (whose name escapes me) took exception to my unbridled enthusiasm and raised her hand once we had stopped singing.

"Mr. Gurstelle", she said, "Mark is singing too loudly, and I can't hear what I am singing."

At this point, my teacher had two alternatives. It is possible that he could have told me to sing more quietly, perhaps softening the blow by reminding me that singing in a chorus required blending with the voices around me. This would have been a devastating blow to a sensitive young man who was already self-conscious about his stature, looks and lack of "coolness". In fact, it might well have caused the end of his vocal career.

Instead, he chose to say "Well, when you can sing as well as Mark does, you can sing that loudly, too." It was all I could do not to break out into a wide grin. I was vindicated and have been singing in choruses ever since, enjoying (almost) every minute, although I have learned to blend my voice with those of my fellow singers. And I have Mr. Samuel Gurstelle to thank for it all.

Mark Pinzur

Ripples

I have always believed myself to be an optimistic and forward-thinking person. When it comes to other people's lives, that is. I feel a sense of altruistic yearning—a sense of applauding someone else's efforts and passing my torch of support to them.

When it comes to my own life, however, I'm sometimes challenged to adopt this optimistic mindset. I isolate, and then beat myself up about all the things that I should do, be and have. Then I'm reminded of the extended hands of loving, kind support that surround me. It fills my cup. These acts of kindness create the bubbling ripples in my heart. Kind influence begets kind influence. A most memorable instance of kindness often comes to mind: a surprising encounter with a special young lady.

Some years ago, I attended a women's personal development conference with my mother and sister. I was ready for that weekend, as I was looking for—something.

Maybe, I just wanted to find myself again. The event was filled with inspiring workshops and speakers, fun activities, games and vendor tables. The hustle and bustle of the event and activities was exciting. I felt like I was in the right place at the right time. It was a bonding experience with my family and in some ways, a bond with the forgotten me. A bridge to the limitless possibilities of my potential.

On the last day of this magical weekend conference, I took a last walk around the vendor tables. With curiosity, I came upon an author sharing and signing her book. Young, with confident wide eyes, her name was Chenae, and she shared how she was able to write and publish a collection of her poems. She couldn't have been older than 25. Wow! I felt inspired by her accomplishment as I too wanted to write a book. It was an item on my bucket list of life goals. We continued to exchange conversation and I graciously continued on my way, after offering many blessings for her continued success. I was not ready to purchase her book as I was down to the last scrapings in my purse, and I decided to continue enjoying the non-monetary events of the conference.

The last workshop, led by a dynamic facilitator, was filled with further inspiration about following your dreams and making your mark in the world, as you define it. He referred to Maslow's Hierarchy of Needs Theory; to achieve self-actualization, you must realize that your dreams can indeed come true. The workshop leader had much expertise on the topic and gave examples of his coaching many clients towards their successes. I was brave enough to share that I wanted to be an author…yet I was hesitant.

The speaker challenged me and gave me the nudge that I can, indeed, do it. One of the other attendees then spoke with a now-familiar voice. It was Chenae, the young lady I had met at her book signing table. She stated the proverbial, "If I can do it, you can do it!" I felt satisfied with that acknowledgement and inspiration, as she had already made a lasting impression on me.

As my mother, sister and I finished the workshop, we found ourselves walking down an empty ballroom corridor, exhausted by the weekend's activities. Lugging conference bags filled with giveaways and purchases, it was time to go home and put all that inspiration, sharing and bonding into actionable steps. Steps that I could use to enhance my quality of life and achievements. As one of the last groups of people to leave, we came across Chenae once again.

I told her how much she inspired me to stick to my dream of being an author. Her dark brown eyes locked deeply into mine as she said with full conviction and repeated the lines, "Again, if I can do it, you can do it!" While her words touched me, she firmly pressed one of her books into my hands. I was astonished and humbled by her gesture. With a twinkle in her eye, like Old Saint Nick, she gave me a wink and moved on her way. I felt so encouraged, and grateful for her generosity.

We inspire, guide, and support each other in many ways. We may never know how far those ripples will go. Her simple gesture, indeed, made a great impact. I never forgot that gesture as I wrote and published my first book. I look back and remember her, and how confident and proud she was of her accomplishment. Moreover, how confident she was of me, insistent that I could do the same, and that I accept the gift of her book.

After publishing my book, a reader told me how inspired and grateful she was, as the book was a catalyst for reconnecting her with an estranged niece. They both read my book, which may have never been written if it were not for the encouragement of Chenae, the young author who inspired and touched my heart.

Akita Brooks

A Touching Response

On January 31, 2018, my life changed forever. I received a phone call from my brother's girlfriend at the time, and she was crying. I could hear my mother in the background. I remember asking what was going on.

The following words changed everything.

"Your brother is dead."

I asked to speak to my mom. All she could muster in between sobs was for me to get there.

The room began to spin. I quickly sat on the floor of my bedroom. My dog sat right next to me and stared into my eyes for what felt like hours.

Those following hours passed by in a blur. Yet, the reality was about to hit me again for the second time in less than 24 hours. We had to meet with the funeral home. I dreaded knowing how much this would cost. More than anything, I hated myself for worrying about the cost, considering the magnitude of who we had lost. My brother Marc. My larger-than-life baby brother. He was always the life of the party.

There we sat, numb and cold from the previous night's events. The older lady from the funeral home talked to us with her gentle voice. She reassured us every step of the way. There were times when my mom would not answer, and just defer to me. Everything flew past me in a blur of coffins, cards, and time. As the funeral home director revealed the cost, I blanked. How were we going to afford this?

The truth is we had no money. My brother had just begun a job, so he had not paid that much into his life insurance policy. I considered opening a credit card and hoping for the best. I figured I could use my savings and pray that it would be enough. It wasn't. During that time, I called different credit card companies to see how much I would qualify for so we could pay for this.

After trying to think and failing to find another plan, a friend called and said, "You might want to think about starting a *GoFundMe* page."

After hours of trying to type the appropriate words, I was able to come up with something to summarize his life. I did not expect much.

I was proven wrong. The power of the internet and the kindness of strangers came in waves. In a matter of merely three days, we hit our goal. Our families did help, but even with that, we were not going to have enough. People shared our page and many donated. The outpouring of messages and overall generosity overwhelmed me. We received prayers and messages of condolence, and people who had also lost a sibling unexpectedly reached out.

Thanks to the generosity and kindness of family, friends and people I have yet to meet, we were able to afford to lay my brother Marc to rest.

Damaris Zayas

Happy

I walked down the halls of the 17-story tenement by the sea that I called home, the harsh neon lights threatening to put me into an epileptic fit. Clutching to my chest 300 neon-pink flyers that proclaimed "These Hands are Educated... Let me rub you the right way!" For 15 years, I had been doing massage. My hands were picky. I was not willing to touch just anybody. As I slipped a flyer under each door, I whispered my witchy little prayer. "Dear Goddess of the Healing Arts, I beseech thee... Please, send me only the people who can receive the magic, accept the healing and pay full price."

I did my due diligence, went home and waited. An hour later, the phone rang. The male voice on the other end of the phone was warbly and weak. Huzzah, the magical spell worked! An appointment was made for the next day.

At 10 a.m., there was a knock. It was showtime. There stood a tall beige man with dark circles under his eyes, and a lopsided smile, his body twisted and bent by the weight of a long life. "The name's Happy", he said with a Texas twang, tipping his head as if he were wearing a cowboy hat. "Happy Franklin."

His name was Happy, but by the looks of him, I could tell that *he* was not. We talked for a few minutes, and I guided him to take off his clothes and lay down on the table.

I left the room to give him some privacy and took a moment to thank the goddess for this opportunity.

When I returned, he was face-down naked on the table. I pulled back the thick white towel which revealed his back. As a seasoned professional, I have seen many things and most every different kind of body, including people with long medical scars, full body tattoos, even missing limbs. But this I had never seen before. He was covered, head to toe with thousands of brown, beige, red and black moles, marks and skin tags ... bruises and booboos, too.

I gasped silently. Unlike the state of Texas from which he came, there were few open spaces on his body... a massage therapist's nightmare. I poured the oil into my hands and placed them on the back of his heart. I took another deep breath and asked him why he was here and how I could help.

To my surprise he poured out his tale, telling me everything that was in his achy breaky heart. I listened, and I listened and listened some more.

"My doctor says I should be taking these anti-depressants, but they don't do a thing. Truth be told, I just don't want to live anymore without Roselyn." He was the kind of sad that drugs could not even touch.

He went on...

"We used to love to go out for long drives up the coast at sunset and go out for dinner." A steak, medium-rare and mashed potatoes with a big bottle of cabernet was their idea of heaven.

"Food tastes like sawdust to me now. Sometimes, I can take a nap during the afternoons, but then I'm awake all night. I feel like I am losing this battle. I just don't know what to do or how to live without her."

She was the love of his life and the life he loved. 60 years of marriage and he would have been grateful for 60 more. My heart broke open listening to this tale of lifelong love and loss. And so, during our sessions, I blurred my eyes and found a way to work around the things that under any other circumstances, I would never have been willing to touch.

Happy started coming to see me weekly and then twice a week for sessions. Like the yellow rose of Texas, finally getting enough water and sunshine, he started to perk up. Something about our unusual friendship made him come back to life.

I am convinced that touch and connection can produce miracles.

Happy was 79 when we met. I was 39. He was a Texas Republican... I am a forever Liberal. He was rich. I was not. We disagreed about politics, religion, guns, and abortion. But the truly important things, we shared in common: our love of people, laughter, integrity, and possibly most important, a passion for good coffee and great smokey, not sweet, BBQ.

During our sessions he told me of the many careers and career changes that he had over the course of his life: from con man to oil man, arts philanthropist to revolutionizing the cuisine on military bases. He had reinvented himself many times and he was very supportive of me changing my career for the better.

Inspired by our conversations, I got clear that I wanted to go back to school and finally finish my college degree. I applied to a small private college in Los Angeles where getting the right answer was not as important as how you think and express yourself. Hallelujah! I was accepted to Antioch University, and let me tell you... It was expensive! I asked my mother to lend me the money, but like so much in our relationship at the time, it was complicated and did not pan out. Not willing to throw in the towel, I went to Happy and asked him to lend me the money. It was hard for me to ask, but as it turned out, it was easy for him to give. He said *yes* immediately, almost as if he'd been waiting for me to ask.

At that point in his life, he had traveled everywhere that he wanted to go, bought everything that he needed, eaten everything he could possibly want to eat and what he wanted now was to help younger people realize their dreams. His timing was great. I was blown away.

Every month, without being prompted, without fanfare or any strings attached, he sent a check. Simple and straightforward.

It wasn't just the money; it was the way Happy *gave* me the money. It was a gift from his heart...clear and uncomplicated. That is what really moved me and created a revolution in my psyche and changed my life. First, I saved his life and then he saved mine. It was a circle of giving as all good things are.

Laurie Ginsburg

Out of Nowhere

H ave you ever met an angel?
In art, angels are portrayed as human beings with wings, messengers from G-d sent to earth.

We call people who act virtuously "angels". They are selfless with their never-ending acts of kindness and compassion.

While I have never met anyone with wings, I have encountered many people who spend most of their time making the world a better place.

This is the story of how one person did just that.

It was July of 2003. My mother had retired from teaching in June. She sold the childhood home where I was raised and moved to South Jersey to be close to my family. My father had died in 1995, and my mom did not wish to live in the house any longer than necessary.

Because her new home was still under construction, my mom came to live with us until it was finished. I had welcomed her help, because at that time my husband was working sixty or more hours a week. That left me alone to fend for myself with an eight-year-old daughter and nine-month-old twins. My babies did not sleep through the night, nor did they nap at the same time. I was constantly holding, feeding, changing and playing with one of them. The word "exhausted" did not begin to describe my physical being.

As part of her transition to a new state, my mom had to obtain a new driver's license. I took her to the local Division of Motor Vehicles (DMV) with my infant son and daughter. Taking them out was a huge undertaking, and one I rarely did on my own.

Unlike many stories you hear about going to the DMV, getting her license went smoothly. It was getting us all home in time for the next feeding that was the problem. I couldn't fold up the double stroller and put it into the car.

After many attempts, the stroller's lock would not release. I had tears in my eyes as something as simple as collapsing a stroller was something I was unable to do. My mom could not get it to close, either.

Then out of nowhere, an older man, who looked to be in his 60s, came walking up to me and asked if I needed help. I told him *Yes, I did.* In a matter of seconds, the stroller was collapsed and ready to be put into the back of my mini-van.

I thanked the man and put the stroller away

I turned around to thank him again, and he was gone. I looked all around and there was no sign of him…except for the lingering smell of his cologne. The same cologne my late father wore.

Was this my father in the form of another person wanting to help his daughter? Or was it simply a kind stranger helping an obviously overwhelmed and exhausted mother?

What I know for sure was that this simple act of kindness has stayed with me for almost two decades. It is the small things that make big differences in our lives.

Marla Feldman

Crab Soccer

T he ground was cold beneath me. *Even a decade later, the memory still lays fresh in my mind.* I stretched my limbs out in front of me, reaching for the first shoe to remove. Our teacher had briefly announced that we would be playing crab soccer, a game where you balance and move on your hands and feet, and for this we were not allowed to have shoes on.

In elementary school, our cafeteria had also acted as our gymnasium, so the ground was even more disgusting. By the end of the class, all of our socks and hands would be coated in dirt and dust. After my classmates' shoes were taken off and placed in the corner of the multipurpose room, it almost resembled a little garbage mountain of footwear. We were told to sit on the black line, so that they could place us into teams. I was squeezed in between two boys, Billy and Jackie (Note: these are aliases). When I was in preschool, I had the hugest crush on Billy.

Billy had hair that could only be described as *Justin Bieber-like*. Jackie, on the other hand, was the guy who was currently holding onto my second-grade heart. I straightened my body into a comfortable position, and looked down upon my socks. My mom had gotten them for me when I started playing basketball earlier in the winter, and since I had been gifted them, they'd been my favorite pair ever since.

"Why do you have those?" I turned to my left where Billy was pointing down at my socks. "They have basketballs on them, and you're a girl. Girls don't like sports."

Stunned at his words I replied, "I play basketball."

"No, you don't," he said, "Who even gave you those?"

At the time my stuffed bunny was named Mr. Bunny, and contrary to popular belief, it was a girl. So the best comeback for a seven year old was, "Mr. Bunny gave them to me."

"What? Who's Mr. Bunny?" he asked, confusedly.

"It's her stuffed animal now, leave her alone, and mind your own business," voiced Jackie, from the left of me.

Evidently shocked at his best friend's brash reply, Billy choked out, "Whatever."

Nobody in all of my fifteen years had ever stood up for me. Not the people who claimed to be my friends one second, then backstabbed you the next. Only Jackie. The rest of the year, he and I were almost inseparable, Jackie saving me a seat at lunch, and always encouraging me to share my made-up stories. I think that part of the reason I've grown to love writing was because of his excitement to see what I would come up with next.

Feelings we had for each other shortly grew into being more than just lunch buddies. The rest of elementary school, we were never put in the same class again, so we grew apart after second grade. Jackie and I still talked on rare occasions. But the years had passed by in a blur, and we spent some years not saying a word to one another, with the only contact between us from our eyes. It was almost as if we were a safety net for one another, because however far we got from each other, we always reconnected.

Phoebe Bellagamba

Crawling Towards Kindness

It's April 2020, and it's Passover. Covid is in full swing, and I have my share of fear about getting it. These were the days when we were instructed to wipe down everything we brought into our homes from the market or stores. I wasn't even going to the market; I had my groceries delivered.

But, I had it in my head that I had to get my grandson's matzoh ball soup, (a grandmother has her priorities after all), and bring it over for Passover. I called the deli ahead of time and was assured that no one else was there. I drove over but discovered a line of people. I felt panic but ignored it, waited in line, and went in to get my soup that I had already paid for.

As they handed me my bag, not all that heavy, in my anxiety I somehow twisted, lost my balance and fell onto my right hip. *Oh no*, I thought. I had a hip replacement in 2019 and was worried I had destroyed it. I wasn't sure, but what I *did* know is that the pain was on a par with childbirth.

This is where the kindness begins. The woman cashier, whose image is a blur in my painful state, comes out from behind the register to help me get up and sit on the bench inside. But I'm not only in pain, I'm also worried. Though I have a mask on, I don't want people so close to me inside with no fresh air circulating. I decline help but register my appreciation.

I call my husband, Michael. He walks over since we live nearby. I crawl out to my car, give him the key, and somehow, he helps me get into the car and takes me home. This is where the next kindness begins.

A man in his 60s whom I've never met (he's the son of another owner in my building), apparently sees me crawling along the walkway and comes out to see if he can help Michael get me into my house. He asks us to wait, then runs inside to get his mother's walker that has a seat on it. He and my husband help me onto the walker, roll me to our townhouse and the two of them somehow lift me up enough to get up the step and into my living room where I collapse on the couch. Did I remember to ask this man's name? If I did, it escapes me now. What I do remember is his kindness.

As it turns out, I did not destroy my hip replacement but fractured my sacrum and my pelvis. With several months of rehab to follow, I totally healed. I'm good, thank goodness and kindness.

When I think back to this time, like with childbirth, the painful images have receded but what remains is the kindness of strangers. I remember the man, whose name I still do not know, who ran out to help me. I also picture the woman in the deli. Even though I did not accept her help, she freely offered it. Two strangers came forth to be of service. Now that's worth remembering.

Laurie Schur

RINGS OF KINDNESS

A Medley of Kindness

◊ ◊ ◊

If beauty is in the eye of the beholder, then it very well must follow that kindness is in the heart of the recipient.

Matthew J. Goldberg

Stories of Kindness

When I was young and living in the ice, snow and insanity of Washington DC, I had two small charges. Constantly navigating the priorities of my career and motherhood, I was often challenged to keep my wits about me.

One particular weekend day, I was at the nearby park with my kids swinging and sliding and goofing off. After a too-short time, we meandered home without fanfare. Not soon after, there was a knock on the door and an unfamiliar face appeared with a familiar leather bag.

Oh gosh, I had left my bag on the park bench and this stranger was at my house to return it. The bag contained money, keys, credit cards and my driver's license. With an enormous sigh of gratitude and relief, I realized my inattentiveness brought me very close to losing my identity and house keys. Instead, this angel appeared and bestowed kindness.

I have never felt so lucky. I attempted to reward him with the money from the bag, but to no avail. Seeing my gratitude was evidently enough of a reward for him.

Kathleen Etxegoien
St. Pete Beach, Florida
◊ ◊ ◊

After a long afternoon of a baseball game with one team and practice with another, my son Spencer and I stopped at Johnny's Hot Dogs for a late lunch. A gentleman sitting next to us at the counter struck up a conversation with us—mostly with Spencer about baseball. When he left, he said to Spencer, "Give me your check."

So, Spencer obliged, curiously. The man politely said goodbye, and that he was going to pay our tab for us because he could tell we were good people. How about that?! I told Spencer we should pay it forward and we did. We left a huge tip for the waiter.

That night, we came home, and guess what was playing on TV? The movie, *Pay it Forward*. Coincidence?

Jean Bobo Read
Loris, South Carolina
◊ ◊ ◊

The best advice I have ever been given by my father is to be a willow. When I have experienced moments of stress or even emotionally traumatic events, I have heard those words ringing in my ears. "Be a willow". Willows will bend and sway and never break. When I start to feel life's challenges negatively affecting me, I stop, take a breath and channel the energy of a willow. Allowing myself to process and release my emotions so that the situation does not end up breaking me.

I have to say that it has taken me some time to write this, because when I sat down to try and reflect on a moment when I received a total random act of kindness that made an impact on my life, I could not recall any one significant moment. Sure, in life I have had strangers allow me to cut in line or I've been given some change, so I didn't have to dig out a penny or two from my purse at checkout. I have had — on a couple of occasions — someone in a Starbucks line pay for my order and for me to pay for the person behind me. I love a good pay-it-forward chain.

Heck, I've even experienced people just waving hello or asking if I needed help putting my groceries in my car. But I could not recall a time that someone made a substantial impact in a single act of kindness. I have had words of wisdom after life experiences that have shifted and shaped how I show up in my world.

So, I have been sitting and reflecting: *Am I missing out because I have not one story to tell?* Or did receiving this prompt give me a gift to sit and reflect on how many beautiful people show up and spread kindness in the smallest of ways? To me, those moments are like a butterfly's wings, or dropping a pebble in a still body of water. Each act ripples out, changing its environment. Thank you for giving me the gift of reflection.

Jessica Mills
San Diego, California
◊ ◊ ◊

It was January of 2003, and I was in the midst of another year as a high school English teacher. While walking downstairs with too much in my hands, I fell, ending up with a tibia/fibula spiral break along my heel. I took off only two days from school as I was in the middle of directing the annual school musical, teaching my regular classes and leading many other class activities.

The main problem? I couldn't put weight on my leg at all so wheelchair-bound, I was. I came into school, really struggling to get around. I did not have Arnold Schwarzenegger-like triceps and biceps. On the last period of the first day, a tall senior class student saw me trying to drive straight. He came over and said, " I got this."

I didn't have him as a student; he wasn't looking for an "A." He just did it and continued to do it to make sure I got where I needed to be for the next eight weeks while I was relegated to my wheelchair. And by the way... were he in my class, I probably would have given him an "A!"

Linda Hammond
Southern New Jersey
◊ ◊ ◊

The kindest act anyone has done for my wife and me enabled us to live where we now reside. BK (before kids), my wife and I were members of a beer-drinking running club (Hash House Harriers). We became friends with an older couple (older to us at the time, they were probably about 50) with no kids. He worked for Boeing as part of the international AWACS delivery team. They owned a small house across the street from Puget Sound in West Seattle.

The completion of a major remodel of their house coincided with a two-year assignment in Europe. They asked us to housesit and to set aside $100/month for expenses. So, we lived in an essentially new house, rent-free, for two years. It allowed us to save a down payment for a house. Then they gave us the accumulated $100/month when our daughter was born *seven* months after they returned to Seattle, and we were settled into our home.

Mark Warner
Seattle, Washington
◊ ◊ ◊

I'd been having a hard day, maybe even a hard week. On reflection, I think I'd been having a hard month, or months... or year. It's all a little blurry.

But that night, my doorbell rang. I wasn't expecting anyone so no doubt worried, briefly, how I looked. I put my eye up to the peephole and saw two female friends standing there. No worries now about hair or makeup, I opened the door.

Hey, I said, or something like it. *What are you doing here?*

We're here for you, they said. They pushed in, grocery bags and wine bottles in hand. They went right to the kitchen. "Have you eaten yet?" they asked while opening cabinets, looking for pots or pans.

Why no, I hadn't. I also most likely hadn't washed the dishes or dusted lately. I'm sure papers were strewn about (they always are), pillows were askew, and shoes were everywhere.

They hadn't asked if they could look through all my stuff and use whatever they wanted... and after a moment's chagrin, I didn't care. They set about their tasks as if they'd been hired to be there. Jeri opened a bottle of wine and Aurora cooked dinner.

They set the table as I drank my wine and *relaxed* on their command. I don't remember what we had, but it didn't matter. We drank. We ate. We laughed. A lot.

And it worked. They accomplished what they'd come to do: make me feel better. I hugged them and thanked them and realized that life is nothing but a series of phases. Some are good, some are just fine, and some really stink. Long or short, good or bad, though, they pass.

Sometimes, it takes something big to move out of a bad phase and into a good one—like a new job, a million dollars, or a clean CAT scan.

But sometimes, all it takes is a couple of friends showing up unannounced to spread a little kindness.

Patti O'Brien
Moorestown, NJ
https://pattiobrien21.wixsite.com/ghostwriter
◊ ◊ ◊

For about six years—ever since our son turned three—our family spent a couple days each summer in Ocean City, New Jersey to celebrate his birthday. We would stay in a humble rooming house called The Sea Wind (sadly, the structure is still there, but it's no longer *The Sea Wind*) that was a good fit for us. It was just two blocks from the beach, and we had a private bathroom, a small refrigerator, and a nice front deck from where we would invariably eat one Chinese takeout meal, followed by cake, ice cream and then a walk back to the boardwalk to work off some of the calories. And sometimes, find even more delicious calories.

On our son's seventh birthday, we broke our little tradition and ate inside this humble, but nice Chinese restaurant. It was our good fortune—literally and figuratively—to be seated next to a couple at an adjoining table. My husband being somewhat outgoing, he either responded to or started a friendly conversation with them.

In the course of this conversation, the usual details— *Where are you from* and *how long are you staying in OC?*, etc.— were exchanged, and we mentioned our family tradition of going to OC around our son's birthday. Our conversation continued casually, in between bites of food. A few minutes later, the gentleman we were conversing with handed a $20 bill to my son, and said, "We want you to have a very happy birthday".

We were delighted but slightly embarrassed, and after thanking him, we knew that he would not accept our returning their gift. So why refuse such a nice, generous gesture?

I am not one to initiate conversations with those who I am not familiar with. But sometimes, these little conversations make the everyday much more interesting, and sometimes, one also realizes that there are a lot of kind-hearted souls out there. In this case, a couple who just wanted to make our son's birthday just a little bit more special. They succeeded.

Ruby Tan
Cherry Hill, NJ
◊ ◊ ◊

My son has grown into a mature young man who is quite self-reflective and appropriately self-confident. I appreciate his continued sharing of his thoughts, dreams, and life with me. Drew demonstrated generosity recently, once again. After seeing a movie, he went outside in the cold rain to get his car and saw a woman lying on a bus bench dressed only in a tee-shirt and pants. My kind son asked her if she would like his hooded sweatshirt, took it off and gave it to her. Later, he told me, "I had a car and a home to keep me warm. She had nothing."

Dr. Ruth Fisher
Los Angeles, CA
www.agiftofguidance.com
◊ ◊ ◊

As we move through our day to day lives, we tend to take for granted the joys of being alive and getting to celebrate so many trips around the sun.

In Judaism, this gift of life, or act of kindness, might be marked when your name is written in the Book of Life for another year.

Can giving a life be considered an act of kindness? I believe the greatest act of kindness is the gift of life, whether this is exemplified by the firemen who ran back into burning buildings on 9/11, or by veterans who risked and lost their lives fighting for our freedom.

As for my own gift of life story, it was that random person who made the hard decision to donate life in the way of an organ donation. A grieving family, thousands of miles away donated a precious gift of life—out of kindness, they made the decision to save another life.

Their darkest day turned into my light, and became the much needed hope for my child's new beginning. Great acts of human kindness during times of deep despair are so hard to comprehend.

Life is the random act of kindness that I celebrate each day, each moment, and with each passing accomplishment in my daughter's life, and I have only a stranger to thank.

With each birthday, and with each family gathering, I look around the table and realize she is here only because of a random act of kindness.

There is no medal, no award, no price tag, no way to fully measure the impact of this gift of life, and the feelings of loss that accompanied this act of kindness. It's meaning goes beyond words, and changes with each new and passing day. A gift of life is the greatest act of kindness!

Harri James
Los Angeles, California
Exboyprods@aol.com
◊ ◊ ◊

(Written to an otherwise anonymous guy in a red truck that paid for my Starbucks this morning—and to all others who choose kindness every day.)

You don't know me. You didn't know that things have been really hard lately, and the last couple days have been a struggle. You didn't know that I almost didn't get out of bed this morning. You didn't know that I was mad at myself for being too emotionally exhausted last night to prep my food for today. You didn't know I was mad at myself for spending money at Starbucks when money is so tight right now. You didn't know I was sitting in my car behind you beating myself up and falling apart inside.

You did something kind without knowing any of that. That act of kindness gave me the hope I needed to keep going. It gave me a little faith that everything will be okay. It put a smile on my face and helped clear my head. It reminded me there are good people in this world. What you did had a profound effect and I wish you knew that.

You never know what someone is going through and how the simplest act could change everything for someone. Always choose kindness.

Amanda Hillman
Merchantville, NJ
◊ ◊ ◊

It's 7:30 a.m., and I have just dropped my handicapped son in his power wheelchair off at the VA hospital. Just another typical Tuesday morning for us.

As I'm pulling out of the driveway at the intersection, I spot a visually impaired young man. The same guy I see frequently walking from the Long Beach VA using his white cane with the red tip to guide him. I imagine he's quite familiar with this intersection as I do see him regularly making the trek across this pretty busy street, usually accompanied by another visually impaired buddy. But on this particular Tuesday, he was alone and there were some complicated construction issues at that very corner: bright pylon cones; big chunks of broken cement; the access ramps were in the midst of being repaired.

I watch as he drags his stick back and forth, to and fro, calculating which way to go. He seems confused, which isn't his norm. Clearly, he feels something is off. I assess how I can abandon my vehicle for a brief moment to help guide him through the barriers to cross the street. I look in my side view and see a line of cars piling behind me, making it unrealistic for me to get out.

And then, I see *him*. A construction worker, a guy in his mid-twenties a bit scruffy looking, with long, dirty brown hair and a bright orange vest, jeans and worn-in, sturdy work boots.

And this is where the typical Tuesday becomes not so typical. The sturdy-boot guy puts down his jackhammer, leaves his work post, and makes his way to this man. I can't make out their conversation, but I see words being exchanged.

I get to witness this moment, this act of kindness. *Sturdy Boot Guy* takes this man by the arm and guides him through this hazardous maze. He proceeds to walk him completely across the intersection. I wipe away tears from my eyes and thank the universe for giving me a reminder of how simple and profound an act of kindness can be.

Ali Wolf

Irvine, California
aliwolf2423@gmail.com

ACT Six

◊ ◊ ◊

"**K**indness in words creates confidence. Kindness in thinking creates profoundness. Kindness in giving creates love."

Lao-Tzu

RINGS OF KINDNESS

Where the Grass is Greener

Saturday, 6:00 p.m.

"Hi!" I said.

I took a step backwards as she opened the door, nearly tripping on the porch in the process and stumbling until I landed on a dead patch of grass on her otherwise green lawn. But my eyes remained fixed on her. Her sparkling high heels and the way her legs shone in the dim light of the hallway. She smirked as I regained my balance and composure.

"Hey."

"Are you ready?" I asked quickly. My mouth was dry and prone to voice cracking when I was nervous. I stepped down from the porch and gestured eagerly to my ancient used car. "Your chariot awaits!"

She shrugged indifferently. "Sure, I guess. Let's go."

I took a deep breath. I guess I had every right to be nervous. After all, I believed that she was the prettiest girl in the entire school. When I told all of my friends that she and I were going on a date, they acted like I had asked Ariana Grande to be my girlfriend and she had said *yes!* Even Jenny, my best friend, seemed impressed.

'Don't forget those gentlemanly manners,' she jokingly texted me as I approached my date's house.

'I won't,' I responded, and I didn't. I opened the car door for her like a gentleman would, and for our dinner, I chose the fanciest establishment in the arsenal of any high school kid: The Cheesecake Factory.

"What a nice young man," an elderly woman said as I gave her my seat in the restaurant's waiting area. Her eyes sparkled as she winked at my date. "You're a lucky girl!"

"Mhm," my date replied, but her eyes remained glued to her phone screen.

6:39 p.m.

"Tell me about yourself." I watched as my date slowly buttered another piece of bread.

"What do you want to know?" she replied.

"Anything."

I didn't want to sound tense, but I knew that the tension was coming through in my voice. I just wanted her to talk to me. Then there would have been less of a chance of me rambling on and on about something she didn't care about and less opportunity for me to voice crack mid-sentence. But so far, she hadn't engaged. I bit my lip and wiped the sweat from my brow. Perhaps she just wasn't the talking type. That was okay, I didn't mind. I just needed *something* from her. Anything to ensure that all of my nerves were worth it.

"I don't know what you want me to say," she said finally, "we've been going to school together since kindergarten. What don't you already know about me?"

I paused to think of a response.

She took a selfie on her phone.

6:57 p.m.

Our food arrived. She had ordered some sort of chicken over pasta. I had ordered a salad. By the time she had finished taking pictures of her meal to post on social media, I was already halfway through my bowl of greens.

"Is it good?" I asked.

She looked up from her phone and shrugged. "It's okay. Probably not worth the money, though."

"Ah." I glanced around, noticing her distinct lack of a purse, wallet, or money. "But you got good pictures at least?" Perhaps it was a bit forced, but it was at least an effort to connect with her about something.

She shrugged again. "Nah, not really."

My phone buzzed in my lap. A text from Jenny.

'How's it going, Romeo? Need a wingman?'

'I need a miracle,' I responded.

'Oh, boy.'

7:06 p.m.

I watched as my date mindlessly pushed food around with her fork as I tried to think of something else to say. My mind drew nothing but blanks.

She and I both glanced up as our waiter approached the table. "Anything else I can get for you today? Coffee? Dessert?"

"I'll take another Shirley Temple," my date said casually.

"And I'll take the check." I voice cracked.

My date smirked. She looked down at her phone. "Oh," she said, "my mom is here to pick me up. Bye!"

Then she was gone.

7:13 p.m.

I sat alone with my thoughts.

I guess she had texted her mom and pleaded to be picked up from the restaurant. I guess that to her, any longer with me would have been torture, as if the meal wasn't torturous enough already. I guess that my string of sleepless nights leading up to this date was all for nothing.

I grabbed my phone and opened my text messages to her.

'Thanks! I had a great time.'

No. Delete.

'Let's do it again sometime?'

Backspace, backspace, backspace.

'What did I do wrong?'

Maybe. At least that one's genuine.

Another text came through. Jenny again.

'You okay? How's it going? Hang in there, I'm here for you.'

A waiter dropped a plate next to me. It crashed onto the floor and broke into several pieces. I put my phone away.

7:18 p.m.

The waiter returned with the bill. Eighteen dollars for her food. Six for mine. Four for her two Shirley Temples. Ten for tip. That was all of the money in my wallet.

I got a to-go box from the waiter and filled it with the rest of her food. She took a few bites of the chicken but hadn't touched the pasta. My lunch for tomorrow, I guess. Then I walked outside and towards the parking lot. Towards my car and towards home, the place where I could forget that this night had ever happened.

7:19 p.m.

An elderly woman was sitting alone on a park bench next to the restaurant. The thought of driving suddenly felt exhausting to me. I sat down next to the woman.

7:24 pm

"Didn't work out, hm?"

I glanced up in surprise. We had been sitting in silence for minutes before this woman decided to speak. I turned and looked at her, immediately recognizing her sparkling eyes.

I sighed. "It did not."

"I knew it wouldn't."

"Well, that would have been good *for me* to know."

She chuckled, casually brushing her foot over the green stalks of grass growing through the cracks in the rock bed. "I hope you walk away from today with a smile on your face. The girl you were with today was not meant for you."

"Obviously," I said, "she walked out on me before I could even drive her home."

"Good. She didn't seem to be that interesting to me, anyway. She wouldn't even look me in the eye when I talked to her. Too consumed with those phones all you kids have." She shooed at me with her hand. "You can do better."

"Can I?" I turned to look at her. "I couldn't sleep for days before this date. I couldn't even think about it without getting nervous and sweating!"

"I'm sure she's quite a catch," the woman mused, "but she still left you like this." She gestured to me, alone and miserable, on the park bench next to her.

"Yeah, I know," I said solemnly.

"Look," she caught my gaze, her eyes still sparkling, "I had a friend tell me this once:

The grass isn't always greener on the other side, it's greener where you water it.

"I don't know who you are, or what you're about. I don't even know your name. But I think what you need is obvious. You need to stop pursuing the people who you wish would make you happy and focus instead on the people *who do*." She smiled once more. "The grass is green where you make it green. But that's just what I think."

I nodded, saying nothing.

We sat again in silence.

7:30 p.m.

My mind was alive. I pulled my phone from my pocket.

'Are you doing anything tomorrow night?'

Sent.

Sunday, 6:00 p.m.

"Hi!" I said.

I took a step backwards as she opened the door, nimbly hopping down to the sidewalk in the process. I knew this front door like it was my own. But my eyes remained fixed on her. Her faded Converse shoes, and the way her legs seemed to dance in excitement in the doorway. She grinned easily at me.

"Hey."

"Jenny… Are you ready?" I asked. I stepped down from the porch and gestured eagerly to my ancient used car. "Your chariot awaits!"

She laughed. "My kind of ride!"

I was no longer nervous. I had found where the grass is greener.

Josh Stehle

The Accidental Plumber

I had seen him before, but he wasn't a regular in our building. He understood English, but wasn't comfortable speaking it. I understood some Spanish but...same. We nodded politely at one another as I entered the building. I assumed he was visiting, or maybe a client of someone as it's an office building with many types of businesses.

He was busy. I could see that, and he saw me coming toward him with my big, heavy bags. Sometimes I look like an old work truck going down the street with its alignment out. The elevator had broken down (for the umpteenth time) and I was going to have to carry my bags to the third floor into my little hair salon as I had expected every time I saw the *OUT OF ORDER* sign . I nodded my usual nod, and he reached out his hands to take my bags. I was surprised.

No one ever asks to help. I guess I looked like an *Aww...she can't lift all that stuff herself* kind of a gal. He took the bags up. He wasn't even working on my floor! I gave him a cold little bottle of water that I kept in my refrigerator for clients. "Gracias" he said. "No, *You,* muchas gracias!" said I.

I went to turn on the water in my shampoo bowl and there was a big leak. Water everywhere. I opened the door, and he was still in the hallway. I yelled down the hall, "Excuse me, do you know anything about plumbing?" I didn't expect that he did. Why would he?

I asked him if he could help me. He came in and saw that I really needed a plumber. He looked at his watch and then at me (looking very nervous) and proceeded to remove the broken part and said he'd be back.

Less than a half hour later, he came back and spent another half hour fixing my problem. It wasn't all that easy. I could see him sweat, and his hands spoke volumes that this was not their first use. It turns out that not only was he working in the building that day, but he actually *did* know plumbing!

When I went to pay him, he shook his head and said, "No problem." I have *never* had a plumber say "No problem", let alone had a person go out of their way to help a stranger and then do it for free! This was just a very kind man, disguised as a worker that just happened to be working in our building.

I was so appreciative of his kindness. And I learned once again to never assume, and to always expect the unexpected.

Lauri Fraser

Wonderful Spanish Hospitality

S ome years ago, I was traveling to France on business, and looked to plan an excursion from there. Spain presented itself as an obvious choice due to its proximity to France, in addition to the warm weather it presents in early autumn.

Spain is a vast country with so much to offer, and at that time, I associated it with great movie directors such as Pedro Almovodar, and Alejandro Amenavar of Spanish-Chilean descent. Other than that, what came immediately to mind was everything from bullfighting to the La Tomatina (tomato festival) to, well, my favorite tennis player, Rafael Nadal.

To that point, I had never been to Spain, and sought an area away from its oft-traveled southern region. I am a shy traveler who likes to keep to myself. Nature and culture appeal to me and I try to focus on local experiences that are authentic. I chose a place that was a little more offbeat yet beautiful, the northern medieval city of Oviedo.

On my trip to Oviedo, I had to take a hop flight which resulted in a baggage delay. Eventually, I arrived at my Airbnb hosts' place well into the night. The host couple didn't speak very much English, and I could not speak Spanish at all. And there was the small matter of my missing baggage.

Slowly and patiently, I had to explain to them about having to land at their place, a good one hour away from the airport, without my belongings. I didn't even have my toothbrush with me. There was no reason for them to fret over my problem. I imagine that most hosts would have asked me to just try my luck the next day.

My hosts knew that I was a bit lost in a new country and that the delay was spoiling my vacation, too. Not only did they invite me into their circle of friends that night to make me feel very welcome, but they also went out of their way to drive me all the way to the airport the following day. They conversed in Spanish with the airport authorities to ensure that I would have no hassles in getting my bag back.

I knew I couldn't have managed this smoothly on my own. And if met with a worst-case scenario, they even offered to help me out with a new set of clothes. I knew they meant it. They certainly didn't have to go that far out of their way for me, but they did. However, we are talking about people with golden hearts.

These wonderfully kind hosts made my trip extra special by taking me to a nightclub where I enjoyed listening to some great Spanish music, eating delicious olives and discussing two icons from their country: Pedro Almodovar and of course, Rafael Nadal.

All in all, my trip to Spain brought me everything I was looking for plus lots of relief, overwhelming gratitude and further faith in humanity.

Azure

My Last Five Dollars

I t's October 1978, the week of my 18th birthday. My dad has been out of town on business and Mom, who hates driving to the airport, asks me to take Dad's car and pick him up. Dad, a soccer coach who is over six-foot tall drives a big car: a Ford LTD station wagon.

So off to the Philadelphia airport I go, stopping for gas along the way. My last $5 nearly fills the large tank. Remember: this is 1978. As I drive over the Walt Whitman Bridge, my inner lightbulb comes on. *Oh My Gosh, I used all my money* (I think, in near-panic mode.) *I don't have the 50 cents to pay the toll!*

My mind keeps racing. How do I get through the toll? I can't run it. The police will chase me. I've never been in trouble. (Note to self: Don't cry!)

Driving towards the toll booth, I search for a police car, but to no avail. Yet, at the bottom of the hill is a phone booth and luckily for me, four men are standing by a disabled car. One of the men is on the pay phone. I pull over and approach them. They can see the panic written on my face.

"What's the matter, honey?"

I tell them my predicament. "I have no money for the toll, and I'm supposed to pick up my dad at the airport."

Their faces light up. "We were going to the airport to catch a flight, but our car broke down. If you give us a ride, we will pay the toll for you."

The car owner is on the pay phone with his wife. He pretty much leaves her to deal with the car as the other guys start banging on the booth exclaiming "We got a ride!" "We got a ride!"

Well, they do have a ride, but...

Yikes! Pick up four strange men? If they don't kill me, my parents surely will. Talk about a dilemma. On the other hand, they're wearing suits and overcoats, and two of them sport fedoras. They each carry a briefcase. *Well, okay then.* Three of them hop in the middle seats of my dad's station wagon, and one sits up front. They hand me two quarters as I approach the toll booth.

They are nice and very appreciative, as we ride together to the airport as if it's just our normal commute. I pull into the airport; Terminal A is their destination. They hop out, thank me and wish me *Happy Birthday.* As a young driver, in a world of pay phones (and no pocket change or police in sight), it was as if these gentlemen had appeared just in time to save my life.

I drive off and before you know it, there is Dad at Terminal B waiting for me. I'm relieved and grateful that Dad didn't witness me dropping off the four strangers, but I end up telling him, anyway. He laughs and says, "This is the perfect example of *One good turn deserves another.*"

Carol Diezel

A Knight in an 18-Wheeler

1982 was a wonderful year. I started a job with IBM on May 10 and married Debbie on May 22. My manager even gave me a week off for a honeymoon, with pay! I had only worked for IBM for two weeks at the time, so this was huge. All-in-all, a great month in an amazing year.

Fast-forward to September. I had left work after just a half-day to get to an appointment with my doctor. I was working at the IBM branch in Dayton, NJ, lived in Burlington Township and my appointment was in Moorestown. I chose to take the US 130 to Interstate 295 route. It was a toss-up between that route and taking the New Jersey Turnpike. I chose the former, as I just didn't want to pay any tolls.

The trip south was uneventful—uneventful that is, until it wasn't. I had just merged on 295 when suddenly I heard a bang. Then, my car got very loud with a scraping sound coming from under the car. I pulled over to take a look.

As a man working for IBM in the early 80s, the accepted dress code for men was a dark suit with a white shirt and necktie. I wasn't a "winged-tip warrior" yet— that would come in a few years when I started working in an IBM sales office—but dressed close to the IBM ideal. I found an old shirt in the trunk of my car which I put to good use as something to kneel on while examining the undercarriage of my car. It didn't look good; the muffler had become detached from the pipe running from the front of the car. It appeared that rust was the culprit.

I had no idea what I was going to do: no tools, no mechanism to lift the muffler and nothing to keep my suit from getting ruined. With no solution in sight, a flatbed 18-wheeler pulled off the road and came to a stop ahead of me on the shoulder. The trucker emerged from his cab with a "Hey there, what seems to be the problem?" I told him, and he immediately took a look.

After his examination, we spoke briefly, also exchanging names and other pleasantries. He mentioned that he probably had something to use to tie-up the muffler to keep it from scraping the road surface. He spent a few minutes in his truck and came back with some uninsulated wire. After a few minutes under my car, he emerged and said that his work would probably hold for a while and at least get me to where I needed to go. I reached for my wallet and pulled out a 10-spot, all I had.

"Nope, no thank you. My good deed for the day. Just please help someone else in need when you have the opportunity to."

I thanked the erstwhile stranger, my knight in an 18-wheeler, and promised to one day help someone else in need. Even better, I still made it to my appointment on time.

Jim McGrath

A Swift Kick in the Pants

"Can I give my mother your number in case she needs something while we're gone?"

I listened to my neighbor Jeff make a simple request at the other end of the phone... and cringed. I was in no condition to help myself since my husband's death, let alone a woman I barely knew. But I realized it would give them peace of mind while they were gone, and they'd been nothing but kind these past few months.

"Sure, you can give her my number," I replied in a casual voice that belied the fear I felt at the thought of his mother actually needing my help with something.

While my twin daughters were at school, I spent most of my day curled up in a fetal ball on my bed with the family dog, a little Scottish Terrier named Izzy. Every few hours, I would force myself off the bed to let her out back to do her business.

A few days later, the dreaded call came from my neighbor's mother, Edith. I didn't know her well. She had moved here from the East Coast and was living with her son's family until they got her settled somewhere nearby. The few times I had met her, she was always well put-together and very formal in her mannerisms.

"Hello, this is Edith Shepard, Jeff's mother." Her proper voice was tinged with a tightness that wasn't usually there. "I could really use your help. I'm in need of some Milk of Magnesia."

My mind immediately started to race. She needed something that would require getting in the car and driving to a pharmacy. The only reason I got in a car lately was to pick up my girls from school. Friends were dropping off meals, so I'd had very little reason to run errands. I was rusty, to say the least. And still deep into my pity party.

"I'd be happy to get that for you."

The words flew out of my mouth before I had a chance to crawl under a rock and hide from this simple task. It took some effort, but I did manage to throw on some semi-presentable clothes and drive to the local CVS.

After wandering aimlessly for several minutes, I found the right aisle. I was shocked to see a multitude of options stocked on the shelf. I remembered Milk of Magnesia as a vile, white, pasty liquid my mother would force down our throats with a spoon when the situation called for it. Now they had it in liquid or pill form, in several different flavors.

I spent what seemed like an eternity deciding between Fresh Mint, Wild Cherry or Original. I tried to call Edith from the store, but she didn't pick up. I needed to make a decision, which wasn't a strong point for me lately. After agonizing over it, I decided to go with the original flavor.

I dropped the little bag off with Edith and the look of relief on her face was palpable. Shortly after, I got a call from her son thanking me profusely for helping his mom get through her discomfort.

It dawned on me that Jeff had done me a huge favor in return. Why did he choose to give her *my* number when there were several other neighbors on the block who would've gladly said "yes"? I think that he knew I was having a hard time and wanted to give me a distraction to take the focus off of myself. If that was their plan, it worked.

I started to find it less frightening to get in my car and drive somewhere other than my kids' school. I began to rely less on friends and started to go grocery shopping for my family. That one urgent call from a virtual stranger in need had given me the swift kick in the pants I so desperately needed to get on with my life.

We were two people who barely knew one another and yet were able to have a positive effect on each other's lives when we needed it most!

Susan Berin

We Are Each Other's Angels

In March of 2020, I managed to play the four shows that I'd booked in Florida, just before the pandemic shut everything down. Despite the common sentiments at the time that this would be a brief pause and that things would soon return to normal, I instinctively understood it would be closer to two years before most people would feel comfortable sitting in a crowd again.

I knew that my 650-mile drive home from Florida would be my last 10-hour drive for a while, and as I reached my steep, uphill driveway, I also understood that I would be home for a long, long time. I was not going be able to make my living as a performer for the time being, if ever again. I was 60 years old, and I suddenly had no income.

What was supposed to have been the busiest and most lucrative year of my entire career began to slowly dissolve, one cancellation after the next. But before I could even panic over how I would pay my bills, friends and fans stepped in. How could it be, that when the entire world was shutting down, and with everything else that was on their minds, anyone would have wondered how Chuck Brodsky might have been doing?

Notifications from PayPal of donations people were sending me started coming in frequently, and checks were arriving in the mail. A miracle was taking place right before my eyes. There were even people who still paid me for shows that had to be canceled. Hundreds of people thought of me and supported me throughout the entire pandemic when I was unable to earn income. I'm still here today because of them.

I wrote a song 40 years ago called *We Are Each Other's Angels*. I was 21 at the time, and although I understood its truth at that young age, I hadn't yet lived it and experienced it. Over these past 40 years I've witnessed or experienced it over and over again. It's become more true with each new day.

Never could I have imagined the power those words would one day have, or how they might inspire other people the way they have. But at a time when I wasn't able to provide for myself, my angels stepped up and kept me going. And when I wanted to release a new CD of my music and I launched a crowdfunding campaign for it, in the middle of a pandemic, my angels rallied around me, chipping in not only enough to pay for the project, but enough to also make a substantial donation to an orphanage in Uganda.

I could tell a million stories of the good and kind deeds I've witnessed or learned of, but the most incredible example of *We Are Each Other's Angels* I could tell is how my angels rose up to stand with me when things looked bleak.

Chuck Brodsky

Lyrics to We Are Each Other's Angels

(Reprinted by permission of Chuck Brodsky)

I hope I see you later, 'cause it's time for me to go
That's my ride that just pulled over, and it sure was good to know you
So go answer your calling—go and fill somebody's cup
And if you see an angel falling—won't you stop and help them up?

We are each other's angels—we meet when it is time
We keep each other going—and we show each other signs.

Sometimes, you'll stumble—sometimes you'll just lie down
Sometimes you'll get lonely—with all these people around
You might shiver when the wind blows—and you might get blown away
You might lose a little color—you might lose a little faith.

We are each other's angels—we meet when it is time
We keep each other going—and we show each other signs.

Thank you for the water—thought I was gonna die out here
In the desert but you quenched my thirst
Let's break a little bread together—I've got a little Manna –
It was a gift
From someone who was passing by and offered me a lift.

We are each other's angels—we meet when it is time
We keep each other going—and we show each other signs.

Goodness and Generosity

In the course of writing my book *Bases to Bleachers*, which is a collection of folks' personal memories that have something to do with baseball, I have learned about the wide range of human behavior that we all can expect to experience as we go through life. The people who are responsive, and those who aren't. Those who are helpful to you, and those who are not, despite every reasonable expectation that they will be. Now, how we deal with disappointment is up to each of us.

Unfortunately, my expectations are high, and I am a personal, proverbial, rollercoaster of emotions, wildly celebrating the *good stuff* and being very down at disappointments. But I had two remarkable, out of the blue experiences—that are far more fun to think about—which affirm the goodness and generosity of people.

As the manager of a co-ed softball team for 25 years, there have been a huge number of people whose names have helped fill out roster and lineup cards. Our longtime slugging and slick-hitting first baseman Vriana brought her friend Hilary to the team. Hilary was a fun teammate, a good player and had a bubbly personality. She played with the Mustangs for one, perhaps two, seasons at most. She soon moved out of the area.

When I began my project, asking everyone I had ever met about their personal baseball memories, I thought of Hilary, as I remembered all the people who had played on our team. A good place to start. I had an old email address for her, and decided to send a message, hoping it would still be valid and my note would find my way to her. It did, she was happy to hear from me and she wrote a story for my book. But she did something far more significant than that. Without even asking me about it, she set up for me (an acquaintance, at best) a Facebook page with the hopes that it would gather attention. I had not even thought about doing that, and certainly did not have the skills to do so if I had.

Whether or not this resulted in a slew of new contacts and great stories is not as important to me as the fact that Hilary jumped into action, voluntarily, to help this person she barely knew. It was a complete surprise, a complete joy and something I will never forget.

I went to high school with Gail. We didn't know each other well at all—we may have had a few classes together, but most of my interactions with her would have been through choir. Gail was extremely popular, in the *in-crowd*, which I most definitely was not. While our interactions were few, she struck me as an incredibly nice, down-to-earth person, traits not always associated with those popular kids.

Gail and I renewed acquaintances at our 40th high school reunion. She was the one person my wife Lynn and I really spent a lot of time talking to, aside from the friends I have always remained in touch with. We were struck by her totally genuine personality, and we enjoyed talking about our lives and our families. When Gail learned that my book had been published, she immediately called her sister, Robin, who is the host of a national show on NPR (National Public Radio). Gail strongly encouraged Robin to interview me. I sent a couple of books to Robin and her producer, and as the 2019 World Series was reaching its final game, Robin interviewed me: she from her Boston studio, and me from the local public radio station where she booked a studio room for me.

I always say results don't matter—it is the willingness of people to help, and the efforts they extend that are important. In this case, those two outcomes meshed gloriously. The interview was an incredible experience. When Robin contacted me to schedule, she noted that the season was coming to an end, and that if the Series went six games, she would book that studio. I spent the several days before that unsure if I wanted the series to go that long, balancing the amazing experience of being on this show with the nervousness I could feel long in advance. The series continued, the studios were booked, and the interview was conducted.

Robin, a polished, professional interviewer, made me comfortable in a split-second. 6 1/2 minutes flew by and I felt like I was talking to an old friend. It was a truly wonderful life experience. This interview also resulted in the greatest boom in book sales, the result that I had hoped for. The experience was so great that it didn't matter whether it did or not... but, well, it mattered.

But this story is far more about Gail. She not only made that suggestion to Robin, but she also reiterated it, continually reminding her, until Robin agreed. How Gail immediately, on her own, helped a barely known high school acquaintance is something I will always remember. We have become good friends since, and that has brought me great pleasure.

Eric C Gray

A Courtly Gesture

I n the rustle and bustle of the large court room for the motion calendar call of civil cases in Kings County, State Supreme Court in Brooklyn, we were scores of attorneys in our suits, toting our brief cases, chatting, awaiting the judge to take the bench. I noticed a lawyer with a recognizable face, a gentle face. *How do I know that guy?*

In an instant, it came flooding back to me. This man saved my proverbial butt perhaps a decade ago when I made my first appearance as a first-year associate in the New York County State Supreme Court in Manhattan.

I was appearing on a discovery motion as the plaintiff. It was me, alone, in an unfamiliar, loud courtroom, facing three defense lawyers with interests inimical to my case, as all cases go. In reflection, I had two barking pit bulls dressed up as attorneys claiming various infractions and delinquencies in the discovery process of my case. The third attorney was not so dramatic; he seemed a little bored, as if he'd been to this movie a hundred times before. We were set to go before the judge where they, collectively, were seeking to have my case dismissed and if not, impose other penalties. Today, a case as such would be child's play to me, but back then, it felt like I would be arguing before the United States Supreme Court.

When my case was called, I stepped up to the bench and it didn't go well. Stumbling over my words...script... or whatever was coming out of my mouth, the judge was not pleased; clearly, she wasn't having it. This judge said she was striking the Complaint. When I attempted to reargue, she actually said, "Step back, counselor" and believe me, she meant it.

I turned around, probably with a crimson face, to descend the few steps down into the gallery and saw the sea of attorneys seated in the benches giving me the look, like either *Whoa, sorry kid, I've been there* or *Wow, you must feel like a schmendrick.*

As I walked to the back of the courtroom, one of my adversaries, the calm one of the three, the man who I now recognize in this Brooklyn court room, approached me. He suggested to me "I think you should ask to be heard again". He explained to me just how to accomplish that: by going up to the clerk of the court who has their place near the bench and request to have the case put back on the calendar. I followed his advice, our case was heard again, and I managed to have the judge's draconian ruling modified.

It is highly unusual for any attorney to help their opponent remedy their case, especially when it certainly wouldn't help their own. Returning to the office, I was relieved when I was able to report a more favorable status of the case to my employer.

Although I had not seen him since that momentous day, the lawyer who helped me on that day was Guy Lawrence of Kanterman & Taub. I walked up to him and said, "Excuse me. Are you Guy Lawrence?"

He looked at me quizzically and replied in the affirmative.

I proceeded to tell him about when we had met in a Manhattan courtroom years ago, and how helpful he was to me. And how much I appreciated it.

He didn't remember it, but somehow that does not surprise me. He had probably done countless similar things for people in his life. That's the kind of guy he was.

Linda Alster Nelson

Holiday Generosity

Many years ago, my family of five fell on extremely hard times. My husband became disabled and could not work. Our primary source of income went from six figures to zero almost overnight. We sold most of our assets to survive and eventually lost our house while we battled for disability status. Because I was the primary caregiver to our three younger, school-aged children, I had not focused on building a career.

When evicted from our home, we moved in with my parents. We got along, but moving a family of five into a three-bedroom house made for cramped quarters. Living almost on top of each other and dealing with newly diagnosed mental illnesses put a lot of stress on everyone. I was working, but only making enough to cover the essentials. We were living on food stamps and Medicare.

With all this going on, I did my best to keep life for my children as *normal* as possible. Christmastime rolled around, and I did not know how to find anything extra to get presents to put under the tree. This only added to my stress.

As the Christmas break got closer and closer, I was called to the principal's office of my youngest's elementary school. This was not a normal event for me to be summoned to the principal's office for any of my children, or even myself. Despite being told that my child was not in trouble, and everything was okay, I couldn't help but be nervous as I walked up the glossy gray stairs to enter the building. By the time my youngest child graduated, we had been a part of this elementary school's family for sixteen years.

I was brought into the principal's office, which was decorated for the holiday season, but very little could put me in a holiday mood while being stressed to my limits. Then, I suddenly noticed that there were several piles of wrapped presents placed around the room.

Once I was reassured (again) that my youngest was not in trouble of any kind, the principal told me about the teachers' holiday tradition.

Instead of the faculty and staff exchanging gifts for the holidays, they pooled the money that they would have spent on gifts for their co-workers. The money went to help a few families in the school that were struggling. I was presented with a mound of wrapped gifts. Not only were there gifts accompanied with my youngest child's name on them, but there were also presents with the names of my two older children, who were now in high school and middle school.

Tears of gratitude for this amazing show of generosity fell from my eyes. I was speechless, unable to find words to express my gratitude for this gift to my children and me. I will never forget the wonderful staff and how they helped to create a normal Christmas during a challenging time for our family. To this day, years later, I still look back at that moment and reflect on those educators' generosity and kindness.

Karen Schober

RINGS OF KINDNESS

ACT Seven

◊ ◊ ◊

I was so blinded I could not see
Thank you for sensing the real me.

Matthew J. Goldberg

RINGS OF KINDNESS

Not-So-Fast Friends

Jack was my father's best friend—ever since they met while scuba diving off a naval base in the late 50s in Yokosuka, Japan. My brother and I were both born there, and I still love seeing "JAPAN" simply stamped in bold on my passport.

My affectionately nicknamed Uncle Jack, strapping and boundlessly athletic, left Japan and the Navy and went on to marry June, an older, more sedentary woman. She was freshly divorced, with four half-grown kids.

I absolutely loved her. She became my "Aunt June" and was wholly different than my stern and serious Southern mother. I used to visit their modern family in glorious Southern California. Their house was always full of laughing teens just in from surfing, eating ice cream, and jumping in the backyard pool in sun-drenched San Diego.

Coming from an isolated horse farm in muggy, buggy North Carolina, I had found my Shangri-la. I moved to California at 18, renting a tiny apartment in an old Victorian house owned by Aunt June and Uncle Jack. He became a west coast father to me, and over the years, I felt comfortable calling him during all hours of the night with medical questions, as he had become a wonderfully patient family physician. Aunt June, a fierce and chatty matriarch, razor sharp, who called me "Honey Lamb", always delighted in my young life stories.

Uncle Jack loved Aunt June dearly, but also found himself connected to someone over the years who was a sporting travel partner, a much younger woman he had evidently met skiing. We all knew about the woman and speculated vaguely for years. *Had he put her through grad school? Bought her a house? Did she live in Seattle?* I remember times when I visited them and stumbled onto Uncle Jack, hidden in a laundry room, speaking on the phone in hushed tones. Once, I heard him say "I love you". It made me feel sick. I hated that burden of knowledge.

June finally swore she would divorce him and even had a "D-Day" note scrawled on their kitchen calendar, but she never went through with it. Her children and grandchildren knew all about Jack's second life, about his weekends *away* that became blatant and uncontested, when he would disappear, like clockwork, once a month. I was stuck in the middle of it all, since my allegiance was from Jack's side, as daughter to his best friend.

I was shocked when June finally died, such a force of nature she had been. I always assumed, somehow, that she would have the last word. Jack was truly wrecked by her death, loving her dearly and patiently taking care of her until the very end. Their love had always been an affectionate and close one, even with his mistress in the mix.

But that didn't stop Jack from promptly marrying Morgan, almost 25 years his junior. I did *not* want to attend the large, lavish wedding but my father insisted. Uncle Jack had called me several times before the wedding to chat and at the end of the call, would always hand the phone to Morgan to say hello. I stammered…and tried. But it felt false and wrong. At the same time, it felt awful to be so chilly to a woman who seemed kind in our brief interactions—one who had done no harm to me personally. Who knows what her side of the story was?

It was like when I watched the documentary film *Winged Migration*. I flew alongside the birds, feeling their flight and plight and left the theatre gushing about viscerally relating to their awe-inspiring lives. My friend quipped, "But what if you were a *fish*?" From the perspective of poor innocent fish, in the same scenario, the film is suddenly a Jaws-like horror story!

So, I decided to put aside my judgment of this woman. I attended the wedding, and found Morgan to be a very tanned, gruff, golf-loving smoker, compared to my healthy-habited hiker and artistic soul, but I had to admit that she seemed sincere, guileless, and very happy. June was no longer here, no longer hurt. I felt I had to let go, and let life move on.

I began to spend a little time with Morgan, and discovered that she was smart, sensitive, and wore her heart on her sleeve. Empathy nudged itself into my reticent little heart and I began to trust her. I shared a few things about my life with her and she responded in kind. She taught me how to play card games and I talked her into stand-up paddle boarding with me, even though she was terrified of the ocean. We traded familial war stories. She was becoming a friend. I began to understand her insecurities, and how she ended up in a long-term relationship with a married man who evidently kept her hopeful, with many promises.

Bit by bit, that tough brittle wall softened in me, and I came to appreciate this new friend-couple, and over the years, I surprised my resolute self and came to truly love Morgan. It started slowly, like when realizing their protective, sincere concern when she and Jack encouraged me to leave a bad, unhappy marriage.

At first, I resisted, but later greatly appreciated their loyalty and support. They just *showed up*. They traveled to watch me perform in a professional play production and joined me and my aging parents on a Caribbean cruise and were, frankly, lifesavers in wrangling my adventurous father, helping me chaperone my ailing but determined 90-year-old Pop as he hailed speeding taxis to take us off the grid, and up perilous dirt roads to see some waterfall or village.

When my father died a few years later, they traveled across the country and stayed for a week, helping my family deal with the funeral, and all that it entailed. It was a comfort having such an old friend of my father there. Morgan was exactly my age, and therefore more of a relatable peer than being around June's motherly, sometimes domineering energy. It proved a different and, in some ways, closer dynamic.

Over the years, Morgan has become a steadfast and loyal friend. She showed up at my tiny apartment and slept on my couch for days after I had a major knee surgery, happily being my driver and bustling around, cleaning the entire apartment. I remember her helping me out of some awkward, sweaty, compromising position, when I was a mess of tears and crutches and pain, and *seeing* her there, holding onto me, trying to make me laugh, this person whom I had once thought I never wanted to *meet*.

They have invited me on trips and that same lovely home, with the ubiquitous ice cream and backyard pool from my childhood, is always open to me. She has graciously embraced me as family, and I know that 1 will grow old with her in my world. I am so grateful for Morgan's unflinching openness to befriend me, which has been such a lesson in humility—of life and its idiosyncrasies—and that by weaving in kindness and acceptance, can bring such delightfully surprising riches.

Alicia Sedwick

Living up to His Name

The first time my father-in-law told me he needed a kidney, I nearly passed out. I was enjoying dinner in Atlantic City with my wife Stacy, my father-in-law Ed, and my mother-in-law Marlene, when Ed dropped the news: he had a rare kidney disease, and his kidney function was down to 15%. He would need to go on dialysis soon, where the average life expectancy is just 5-10 years.

The blood drained from my face, and it took me a good ten minutes to recover. Once I was able to come back to the dinner, we started talking next steps. Ed was already on the kidney donor list, but that could take years. The best solution was to find him a living donor.

Ed and Marlene had already decided that he wouldn't accept a kidney from either of his two daughters. Additionally, his other son-in-law had health issues that disqualified him. That left me. In an incredibly cruel twist of irony, though, I would be diagnosed with a kidney stone the very next day, which meant a kidney donation would be highly risky (if I got another stone, it could destroy my remaining kidney).

And so it became apparent that the donor would have to be a friend or, less likely, a stranger.

We began throwing feelers in all directions. Stacy, her sister Rachel, Rachel's husband Eric, and I created a Facebook page to get the word out. We invited everybody we knew to the Facebook page and asked them to share it with everybody they knew. Eric got custom t-shirts to wear that directed people to the page. Ed's synagogue put out word that he needed a donor. Each of us asked our friends and people we hadn't talked to in years if they would be interested.

But we soon found out that it wasn't as easy as just finding a generous soul. We had a lot of generous people in our lives and our communities, but becoming a kidney donor is *difficult*. All of our volunteers and leads were quickly disqualified due to age, blood type, health, or some other precondition. It was very, *very* frustrating.

So I expanded the search. I Googled celebrities that had received kidney donations and tweeted at each of them asking for help to get the word out. I asked for a favor from actor Sean Astin, whose family I knew from college, and he sent out a message to his 400k+ followers. I then tried to use THAT message to catch the eye of his co-stars on *Stranger Things* (the only thing that accomplished was earning me a spam warning from Twitter).

Finally, I asked the University of Michigan community—where I went to law school—for help. That's how I found Dave Heal. Or more accurately, how Dave Heal found us.

The Michigan community prides itself on its generosity, and so when I asked Michigan sports blogger Ace Anbender to retweet out a plea to the Michigan community, he did so with the message "I've learned never to underestimate the Michigan community, so let's see if there's someone out there..." Ace would know better than anybody, as the Michigan community raised tens of thousands of dollars to help him through a health crisis. It was a shot in the dark, but one with reason for hope.

Dave Heal saw the message and contacted me. Dave had already tried to donate a kidney to a stranger, but was told months later that the stranger had found a donor, so "thanks, but no thanks." He was ready to try again. More importantly, he was relatively young and healthy.

He filled out the form and began the long and daunting donation process. In order to donate, Dave had to undergo numerous tests. They checked his health (it was good). They checked his compatibility (he was compatible). They asked him hundreds upon hundreds of questions about his mental state, his motivations for donating, if he understood the risks, etc. They did countless blood tests and had him pee in cups—420 times (by his count). He did it all without complaint.

Meanwhile, Ed's doctors mostly kept him in the dark. They did so for an obvious reason—they didn't want to get his hopes up. It's a BIG deal to donate a kidney and a lot has to go right for a willing donor to be able to donate to a willing recipient.

I wasn't limited by these professional ethical considerations. I was regularly messaging Dave on Twitter and checking on him every few weeks. I learned that he was having to fly out to Pennsylvania (he lives in Colorado) for testing, so we kept offering to cover the costs of travel (you can't legally pay somebody for a kidney, but you *can* cover the costs of donating). He refused every time.

Ed was eventually told that they had somebody lined up (they didn't tell him who, but we knew it was Dave) and things were looking good.

Then Covid-19 hit, and the world shut down. Hospitals were overrun by gasping patients and organ transplants were put on hold. We would have to wait it out.

During this time, Dave could've changed his mind at any moment. And who would have blamed him if he had? The world was combating a strange, deadly disease that killed thousands of people every day, and we had precious little information about how it was spreading or how it affected the body. It would have been natural for Dave to question whether he wanted to voluntarily undermine his own health to help a complete stranger.

He never wavered. Or, if he did, he never told me.

As society started to get a handle on the novel coronavirus, hospitals began to open up again and transplants started to get scheduled. We were back on course.

Then they found a nodule in Dave's lung. There was a decent chance it was cancer. Dave once again had a good reason to back out. He didn't. And fortunately, it turned out the nodule was benign. Once again, we were back on course, and this time there were no more obstacles.

A few months later, the surgery was finally scheduled. Ed and Dave were prepped and put into isolation. Dave would have his kidney removed in Colorado, and they would fly it into Pennsylvania. In the days leading up to the procedure, I was regularly messaging Dave to make sure everything was good on his end. On the day of the procedure, he sent me a picture of himself in recovery with his kidney in transit. Both surgeries went off without a hitch and when they put the kidney into Ed, it began working immediately (which we were told is unusual). Dave had given Ed a very, very healthy kidney.

Ed's life immediately improved. While he now has to take dozens of pills each day, it's a small price to pay for getting off dialysis. His energy picked up and he began to feel like himself again. Dave also recovered nicely, and was able to get back to his usual routine within a few weeks.

A couple weeks after the procedure, we had a Zoom call with Dave, his girlfriend, and our family, which was the first time Dave had ever talked to Ed. Dave and I also interviewed for an article in the Michigan Law paper, which is how I found out that my consistent outreach to Dave clued him into the fact that Ed's future depended on him. Other than that, though, communication has been relatively sparse. Ed wants to meet Dave in person and take him on a trip to New Orleans or Las Vegas, or some other destination as a token of his immense appreciation, but as far as I know that trip hasn't been scheduled.

In other words, it appears that Dave Heal was very content to go through the incredibly arduous process of donating a kidney to a complete stranger without expecting anything in return. The story seems too good to be true, with a man named Heal adding years to Ed's life just because he could. And yet that is exactly what happened.

Dave Heal truly lived up to his name.

Jeremy Garson

Equinox

The call came in the middle of the night, jarring my husband and me out of a sound sleep in our Mexico City condo.

"AY-kee-noxe is very upset," said the young veterinarian with a thick Spanish accent, endearingly mispronouncing the name of our gray cat, Equinox. "He can't breathe." He sighed heavily. "He cannot continue like this. Can you come?"

I sat up in bed and glanced at my watch. 3 a.m. What kind of vet is at work at 3 a.m.?

Bob and I had arrived in Mexico City, altitude 7,340 feet, just one week earlier. It was the latest stop in our nomadic retirement. We had road-tripped for a week from Pennsylvania with Equinox (*Noxy*, to us) and our other cat Kaylee in the back seat of a Toyota Tacoma, making stops in New Orleans and San Antonio to break up the trip for the cats. We had barely unpacked and started exploring Mexico

City when Noxy started acting strangely, lying down in a dining room chair and not moving even to eat. When he did finally muster some energy, he used it to slink into his carrier in the laundry room and lay down, head in his paws, panting. We frantically searched online for a vet who could speak English, and ran with the cat to Londres Veterinary Hospital, four blocks away.

The young doctor looked like he was barely out of veterinary school. He had a serious face, thick-framed glasses and wavy black hair. I had to hold myself back from smoothing down the cowlick on top. He examined Noxy very gently. "His heart doesn't sound right," he said. "I think he needs an X-ray."

Later, he showed us the black-and-white picture of Noxy's heart, its walls thick and barely moving. "I'm going to bring in a cat cardiologist."

Noxy was diagnosed with hypertrophic cardiomyopathy, a genetic condition in which the heart muscles progressively thicken. It often shows no symptoms until it is quite advanced. For Noxy, the stress of the road trip combined with the extreme altitude of Mexico City had delivered the double whammy that overtaxed a heart we didn't even know was damaged.

Our sweet gray tabby was in the hospital for two days, put on oxygen, and tethered to wires delivering vital fluids. He just lay there listlessly, as his breathing became increasingly labored. Back at the condo, Kaylee lay alone on the couch without her companion, undoubtedly confused; the two were accustomed to napping side-by-side.

The sweet young vet brought in the top kitty heart expert in Mexico's capital, and tried every possible treatment to relieve Noxy's symptoms. He even ordered in a hyperbaric chamber. But before it arrived, Noxy took a turn for the worse. It was time to say goodbye and give the sick cat peace.

Of course, it was heartbreaking. When we arrived at the veterinary hospital at 3:15 a.m., I noticed a beautiful woman in a party dress standing in the darkened lobby before we sprinted up the stairs. She smiled at us sympathetically as we passed. The vet was waiting in an examination room, also red-eyed, stroking Noxy's neck. The cat lay on the table, oxygen puffing into his nose and mouth from a tank.

I noticed that the doctor's pupils were dilated, and he was wearing a rumpled suit. He was sweating.

It turns out the woman was his girlfriend. They had been out celebrating her birthday, dancing in a bar, when he got the call that our cat was in distress. He came to the veterinary hospital in the middle of the night so he could examine Equinox, call us, and then support us through our difficult hour.

That included giving us time to call our college-age kids, one in Vermont and one in England, so they could say goodbye to their beloved pet. That included waiting for Bob to run back to the apartment and get Kaylee so she could see her companion one last time, to at least have an idea why he disappeared. That included letting us hold our boy as meds were delivered to still his barely beating heart. The vet did it all with a tearful smile, apologizing numerous times for his slightly inebriated condition. And his girlfriend waited patiently downstairs, giving us the time and space we needed.

The young vet's kindness helped make an excruciating experience a little better. His big heart helped us manage the failure of Noxy's. He had gone above and beyond to try to save our cat. He cried with us as her heart stopped beating. I wish I could remember his name. I'll never forget his kindness.

Lisa Hamm-Greenawalt

Life and Sacrifice

It was a dreary, cloudy day with a hint of warmth left over from the remnants of summer. My partner and I were employed by NDRI (National Diabetes Research Interchange—now the National Disease Research Interchange)—a not-for-profit service that facilitated the donation of organs to researchers in the diabetic field and later, in other fields of biological research. We were being sent to a hospital where we were to harvest a pancreas for research.

We parked in the visitor lot and faced an aging, four-story, solemn-grey brick building. The parking lot was wet from a morning rain and puddles dotted the rutted blacktop that led to the front entrance. My partner carried a large red and white oversized Styrofoam container retrofitted with a plastic handle that allowed it to be carried like a shopping bag. I was carrying a four-liter grey cryogenic Dewar storage container, three-quarters filled with sloshing liquid nitrogen.

The front entrance was all grey oxidized aluminum and foggy glass façade and bespoke of passive neglect. Passing through the three-part revolving door that creaked and moaned, it made a swishing sound as we pushed against the partitions. The foyer displayed a well-worn Congoleum grey and red tile that sported an obvious track to the main semicircle reception desk. A middle-aged woman, dressed in a high-starched white uniform, immediately focused her attention to us. She had a kind face and a genuine smile that looked out of place with her brown hair done up in a tight bun on the top of her head. Her hospital identification card was laminated and attached to a blue and white lanyard around her neck, and hung below a frilled pink scarf tied loosely around her neck. It read, "Brighton, Melinda". Her picture was of a younger face sans wrinkles and a lack of grey hair.

"Good afternoon. Are you here for the transplant?" she said while placing a rather ragged sign-in booklet and a pen facing us. "Please sign in."

"Yes, we are with NDRI for the organ donation that is to start at 2 o'clock." I said as I picked up the pen and printed my name and signed in with the date and time. My partner put down her container and signed in.

"You go up the elevator," Melinda said pointing to a bank of two elevators, "…to the second floor and follow the yellow lines to Operating Room Number Four." Her smile never faded, and her eyes seemed to sparkle as we moved toward the elevators.

My partner pressed the *Up* button and we both put down our containers to wait for the elevator. A soft ding, and the arrow light went out when the left elevator began to silently open. We entered and pressed a rather well-worn *Number 2* button and the doors closed slowly. A slight lifting sensation and then the elevator car shuddered a bit and came to a stop. The doors opened a few seconds later where we immediately saw five different colored lines, about three inches thick, leading out from both elevators. We followed the yellow stripe down the hall and turned left to a clean but dimly lit corridor that led to a soft-colored blue swinging door that had a black number 4 on it. We hesitatingly pushed through the door and were met with a nurse completely gowned in surgical light-green scrubs, already masked with a white cheesecloth facemask that covered her nose and mouth.

"You are from NDRI?" she said crisply, and led us to a small side room. "Please put your containers here," pointing to a place on the floor, "wash your hands here and gown up, I'll show you what to do."

We followed her and she led us to the scrub uniforms, and showed us how to put them on over our shoes and clothes. She gave us cloth *hats* to cover our hair and surgical masks. Then, she helped tie off the scrubs in the back. Next, she took us to a large stainless-steel sink where she showed us how to scrub and wash our hands. She gave us crisp, starchy towels to dry our hands and told us to put our hands in front of us. She expertly placed light-blue rubber gloves over our hands and pulled them over the sleeves of our gowns.

"Don't touch anything except your transplant box and Dewar container. We will place the donor's organ in your transplant box at the proper time. I will show you where to stand in the operating room."

She then took a white towel and poured alcohol on it and wiped down both containers and the inside of the Styrofoam container. She gave us the containers and pushed through another set of swinging doors into a brightly lit operating room. We placed our containers on a stainless-steel cart next to the far wall. The operating room had bright yellow walls and sparkling clean green linoleum floors. A bright domed light was suspended from the white acoustic tile ceiling and many other gowned people entered, holding up their hands in front of them. Some of the gowned people held transplant boxes with giant letters on them, each indicating a body part: HEART, LUNG, KIDNEY and EYES.

Suddenly, there was a shift in the crowd as the patient was wheeled in along with a heart-lung machine that made a rhythmic hissing noise that was penetrating and pervasive. I could just see the bare arm of the young woman on the gurney. It was a white arm that was slightly pink. Her fingernails were painted red. I detected a whisp of blond hair sticking out from the surgical cap of the patient. Her mouth and nose were covered with a greenish, clear mask and fogged over with each beat of the machine.

Just then, the swinging doors opened, and four more people came in. One was clearly the head surgeon, and one was a gowned-up priest with his clerical white ivory shawl over his surgical coverings. The last two were an older husband-and-wife couple, clearly agitated and looking like they felt out of place. Grey hair was seen sprayed below the surgical caps and the man had his arm tightly around his wife's shoulder, holding her close to his body.

The room was silent, save for the gently breathing machine that softly hissed with the rise and fall of the woman's chest on the operating table. The surgeon took his place and several gowned people opened up a space next to the young woman whose breathing sounds dominated the venue. The priest moved forward, gathering the two elderly figures along with him to the side of the table where the young woman slept, her eyes closed to the proceedings around her.

A tear was formed in the old woman's eyes, just above her face mask, and she huddled closer to her husband. He tilted his head to touch the top of his wife's head and closed his eyes.

The priest began to speak. I could not hear exactly what he had to say, but the timber of his voice and the slow cadence was comforting, nonetheless. His voice rose and I could now make out what he said.

"At this tragic time, we are in the presence of God and his children. Joan and Michael *Smith* have graciously made the decision to turn a tragedy of their daughter Helena's accident into a blessing for many people who will be able to live from her donated organs. Joan and Michael are true Christians that in their time of grief looked out for others by donating her organs to those that cannot live without her sacrifice. In the name of the Father, the Son, and the Holy Spirit, we sanctify these gifts to others and may we all say, 'AMEN'."

The entire room reverberated with the AMEN and the wife turned her face to the husband's chest and her shoulders heaved in a series of sobs. For a moment, even the breathing machine was still.

The priest gathered the husband and wife back from the table and the surgeon took his place by the left-hand side of the patient. A scalpel was handed to him, and he made an incision in the center of the chest. From my vantage point, I could not see this, but it was clear that the key part of the operation had begun. Soft orders for surgical implements were audible and one of the gauze pads that was used to stanch the blood flow fell to the ground near the table. Soundlessly hitting the floor as the surgeon commanded,

"Take her off the machine."

The arm that I could see went from pink to white in what seemed like an instant. The surgeon placed the heart in a transplant box with the grace and precision that matched the solemnity of the moment. Each organ was removed and placed in a different box, the flurry of the operating room like some well-choreographed ballet, moving without a hitch. The transplanted organs were whisked out in white boxes at a crisp pace and there were fewer and fewer people left in the operating room. The pancreas was the last organ to be removed, and one of the nurses carried it over to our transplant box and placed it inside. I removed the cap of the Dewar flask and poured the liquid nitrogen over the light pink organ until the box was half full. We closed both containers and began to walk out of the operating room. The surgeon was stitching up the body and the priest stood consoling the parents as they both sobbed silently while holding each other tightly.

As my partner and I went through the doors and removed our surgical uniforms, we were silent. The passage of the last few minutes has been indelibly tattooed on my memory ever since, as I realized that life sacrifices are made every day, and I had just witnessed this unfold in real time.

Steve Levin

A Long-Lasting Note of Gratitude

O ur college years are life-changing, and that was certainly the case for me. My own alma mater, SUNY (State of New York) Brockport, played a huge role in my life, thanks to the efforts of the Academic Success Center, that coached me through the college process; the faculty and students, who took notes for me; and my roommate, who pitched in and also made me laugh.

Let me give you some background to put this story in perspective. The year was 1979, and I had just transferred to Brockport from the University of Buffalo. My first year in college was less then successful, as my first school was not prepared for a student who had dyslexia and an auditory response problem.

Brockport welcomed me with open arms. That is not to say it was easy, as this was new territory for both the college and the faculty. However, even if it was begrudgingly at the outset, they were willing to work with me. This included identifying students who would be willing to share their class notes. I had NCR (No Carbon Required) paper which allowed me to give my notetaker my special notebook. This way, once class was over, we had two copies. These students were great, and when they knew someone else was counting on them, they never let me down.

I needed to take oral exams. The only way I could make this work with the professors was never to miss class. I could not ask the professors to give me oral exams and not respect their time. Professors at the school accommodated me, and this made all the difference in my college experience.

However, since I was the only one taking the exam in this non-traditional way, most of the teachers just gave me a B. They knew I was prepared, however, that didn't mean they were going to say that I demonstrated A-knowledge.

I had a friend who wanted to be my roommate for my first year at Brockport. Tom Long was a classmate of mine from Brighton High School, one year behind me. I told Tom that he would have to put up with my other roommate. He was not happy until he met Bob the Deer. Yes, it was a deer head! Tom figured we could have fun with this development.

Tom did not know that I had a different learning style, but it became obvious pretty quickly. I had a yellow tape recorder, given to me by the Library of the Blind, who provided my books on tape. I listened to all my textbooks.

They read every word and explained pictures and charts. One of the features was that I could adjust the speed of the recording so I could make it go faster. It was not long before Tom would lend his support. That took the form of reading my class notes into a tape recorder. This system worked great, even if it was time-consuming.

Although helpful and kind, Tom did have some fun at my expense. Keep in mind, he was 18 and bored, so while reading my notes, he decided to spice things up by adding a few pages of Penthouse Forum during one of his tapings. It was pretty funny, and no harm was done.

I became a successful college student, earning a Bachelor of Science in Communications Studies in three years, with a 3.0 GPA. School was not just about academics. I was told when I came to SUNY Brockport to get involved in campus life, and I took the message to heart. I took part in track and field for three years and was even captain my senior year. I wrote for the school paper and was resident advisor for two years. The skills learned at Brockport opened many doors in my life. Before I left, I was even featured on a brochure about being a successful transfer student.

The confidence gained at Brockport made me believe I could be successful at whatever I put my mind to. This included getting my Master of Science in Physical Education and Sport Management from Ohio State University and my Doctor of Education in Sport Management and Leisure Studies from Temple University.

Taking my lessons learned in my education, it was time for me to apply my knowledge to my own career. I started as an Assistant Professor at Tulane University, staying for three years. Today, I am a Professor at the University of Dayton, where I've been for 26 years and counting.

It has been a rewarding journey, largely built on my experiences as an undergraduate. As of today, I have written 60 refereed journals and 144 non-refereed articles on a variety of subjects. However, writing an Op-Ed for USA today on learning disabilities and the NCAA led to going to New York City, where I was featured on *Good Morning America*. I was interviewed by Charlie Gibson, and the introduction started with, "We have with us today, Dr. Peter Titlebaum, Director of Sport Management from Tulane University, who had a learning disability." My response was, "I still do." I just learn differently. It was rewarding to see how far I had come in my career.

These are just a few of my accomplishments, but this only could have happened because SUNY Brockport took a chance on me and saw my potential. I am eternally grateful as I am approaching 40 years since I graduated.

I kept many relationships with teammates, coaches, professors, and administrators, all of whom impact my teaching today. It used to surprise my wife Deb when I would get a call and she would ask who it was, only to be told that it was a student of mine from years ago. She would tell me that this was not normal, based on her own experiences. I would reply that it was just the way I was taught. I keep people in my life from my past as they were with me during my journey.

Tom Long was an important part of the college experience and became part of my family. Even though he was only my roommate for one year, nobody could make me laugh like Tom. This person made sure you did not take life too seriously. This was extremely helpful with the stress of college. We stayed close, and long after college was over, this was a gift.

Have you ever felt the need to apologize for something you did, even though at the time, you were not aware it was an issue? I took part in my Brockport graduation ceremony in the school stadium in 1982. Since my roommate was a stuffed deer head (Bob the Deer), I brought him with me to the ceremony. He did have his own mortar board, and this way, my parents could find me among the 3,000 graduates.

Rumor has it that SUNY Brockport made a rule about me after I left college. No, it was not in my name, as that would really be awkward. The new rule was that students could not bring any uninvited animals into the stadium for commencement exercises. I never intended to offend anyone, and if anyone from my alma mater is reading this, please accept my belated apology.

Peter Titlebaum

Texas-Sized Generosity

My story starts in 2019, which you may faintly recollect as the year before Covid, or the time when we last could touch our faces in public. I cover the Texas Rangers as a beat writer for *Last Word on Baseball*. The first game that I worked in person was on June 4, 2021 against the Tampa Bay Rays.

As a lifelong baseball lover, I have a dream job, but it does come with challenges. One thing I deal with every day is Cerebral Palsy. CP affects my balance, coordination and motor skills. The main challenge this brings to my job is that of getting to and from the ballpark, Globe Life Field, at least 80 times a year.

To get around the challenge of not driving, I always went back and forth using Lyft. However, Lyft has provided its own obstacles. After each game, it was very difficult to lead the driver to the dark, obscure spot where I exited the ballpark. This caused many delays and uncertainties over the course of at least 15 games.

One evening after working the game, I again called for a ride home with Lyft. (Where I work, Lyft is pretty much the only game in town.) The driver, as usual, had their share of difficulties finding me. After about 25 minutes, they finally were able to locate me.

I found out that this Lyft driver also happened to be a security guard at Globe Life Field. Despite this, he still had difficulty locating my obscure spot. He eventually found me that night and drove me home. On the way home, I told him that I depend on Lyft a lot due to my having Cerebral Palsy. I also told him that drivers have a lot of trouble finding my spot outside the ballpark on a nightly basis. He said that he could only imagine how frustrating that must be.

On that drive, the Lyft operator, Duane, and I commiserated about the state of the Texas Rangers. I told him that I'm a credentialed Rangers beat writer for *Last Word*. When I mentioned that, I could almost see the wheels of kindness working within Duane's mind.

After a little more small talk, Duane surprised me with a most generous offer.

"How about this. I'll meet you here about 45 minutes after each game's conclusion (he has other duties to attend to after games) and drive you home."

I was shocked, as well as relieved.

A millisecond—not even two—later, I accepted his offer.

So out of the goodness of his heart, Duane drove me home, as promised, in his silver-and-gold minivan for the rest of the season. For free! He has been such a big help, as he has cut my Lyft expenses (it costs nearly $40 roundtrip......for a 2.5 mile ride, no less) in half! I offered to pay him, but he wouldn't let me.

Duane helps me with my walker if and when I need to use it (Note: I almost always need to use it after each night game) and talks baseball with me during each trip. What could be better?!

Since that night in late July, 2021, Duane has become not only my driver but also a good friend. So from the bottom of my heart: Thank you, Duane!

Nate Miller

A Dash of Kindness

After four years of marriage, we finally moved into our first house in Old Bridge, New Jersey. I was a supervisor for a very successful grocery concern. On the mortgage application, they said my employment future was excellent.

Within three months of our move, the company announced cutbacks and I got swept up in a 600-employee reduction. It took me another three months to find a new job in Manhattan. Between the travel and the expense of it, I found another part-time job, and then a weekend job just to keep our home.

Our daughter was born in November of 1968, and the school cut-off date for kindergarten was December. We were informed that if she attended nursery school, they would waive the cut-off date. In order to lower the tuition of the nursery school, my wife volunteered to help raise funds. She didn't drive, but one of the other parents drove her. That other parent was Dr. Herbert G. Dash, a dentist in Old Bridge.

When I needed dental work, my wife let Dr. Dash know of our financial situation. He said I should make an appointment and we could work out payments. On my first visit, Dr. Dash asked if I was handy and offered me the opportunity to repair some broken stairs in the back porch of his office building to pay for the dental work—which I did. He put my work hours towards his bill. He was an excellent dentist to boot, always joking to make the visits enjoyable. For example, when my mouth was full of instruments and dental gauze, he would ask me ridiculous things to say like The Pledge of Allegiance.

My wife had discussed our struggles with Dr. Dash, and how hot it was since we did not have air conditioning in our house. Amazingly, just a few days later, a full-sized AC unit appeared on our doorstep. The good doctor said it was doing no good in his garage since he had installed central air in his house.

In time, we became very good friends, spending a lot of social time with the doctor's family.

One morning a few years after I was back on my feet, there was a news report that three men had died in a private airplane crash departing the local Old Bridge airport. I thought I heard my dentist's name. But no, it couldn't be. I called his house, and all I heard was crying on the other end. What a deep tragedy.

The funeral was held in Manhattan at the Riverside Funeral Chapel on Amsterdam Avenue. That was where

VIPs were mourned. There were eight hundred people in attendance. From the many people who eulogized Dr. Dash, I realized that his kindness was abundant. His was the most kindness my wife and I ever experienced.

Elliot Dennis

Play It Forward

I once heard someone say that a true act of kindness is when we do something for a person who will not be able to pay us back. Otherwise, there always seems to be some kind of string attached to our gesture, an unspoken expectation of getting something in return.

In my life, I have experienced situations where someone did something to help me or where I did something to help someone without expecting anything in return. Perhaps, the best one for me happened when I started my first job.

I am a musician. I had lived with my parents way past my high school days, and to be honest, I had no idea about what I was going to do with my life. But I had been studying music. More specifically, I had been studying electric bass with a great teacher. My teacher lived in a city which was a one-hour commute from the town where my parents lived.

One day, my teacher said to me, "I have been offered a great opportunity to play with a well-known band. But it means I have to quit my gig at a top-40 cover band. We play four nights a week, three to four sets a night, in a couple of night clubs. Occasionally we also play at wedding receptions and parties. They will need a bass player when I leave. Would you be interested in taking my spot?"

As you can imagine, I was only 19 and the fact that my teacher thought so highly of me to recommend me as his replacement? Well, I was on Cloud 9. How could I refuse!

This would mean that I would move out of my parent's home, get my own place and have my first job. As a musician, no less!

But I was very nervous. Frankly, I was scared, and I expressed this to my teacher. He assured me I would be fine, and told me not to worry. He promised to help me.

I learned and rehearsed the repertoire with my teacher, and he even went with me to the audition (which I passed!), then went with me to the clubs for the first few weeks just to make sure I got the hang of it. He would even play some of the songs I was still struggling with. He observed and took notes as to what I needed to work on. The bandleader was also very patient with me since I was not a pro who could just jump in and replace my teacher right away. True, they had nobody else, but they were willing to give me a chance.

My teacher did all of this without getting paid for his time, and simply because he wanted to help me succeed. Granted, by taking his old gig I was solving a problem for him. But all he did to help me succeed is just unheard of. He truly went above and beyond.

I said to him, "I am so grateful to you for all of your help. How will I ever be able to repay you?" And he replied, "You don't have to. When I was younger someone helped me the same way I helped you. Someday you'll be able to help someone else. Just pay it forward."

My teacher had basically launched my career as a professional musician, but he did more than that. He instilled in me the need to help others, which eventually led to my becoming a music teacher. And yes, as a musician, I have been able to "play it forward" to the next generations.

Antonio Gandía

The Blessings of Sunflowers

An act of kindness can often come from the most unexpected situations.

Last week, I was walking through the courtyard of my apartment building to my car when one of my neighbors was just coming in from shopping. We smiled and said "Hi" at the same time. I said, "That's a beautiful hat you're holding."

Leticia said, "Do you like it?"

"Yes, where did you find it?"

"I picked it up as we were returning from our home down in Mexico. We were down there for a whole month."

"Did the family go with you?" I asked.

"No! It was a real vacation. Just the two of us, Nico and me."

Leticia and her husband live with their daughter, son-in-law and four young grandchildren. She cares for the children while the other adults work during the week.

"You do look rested and relaxed. And your new hat is beautiful. I love the embroidered sunflowers on the black velvet brim. It's a riot of bright colors; the golden petals, the brown and black seeds in the centers and those leaves with forest and lime green embroidery. You picked a good one." At which point Leticia held it out to me and said, "Here, I want you to have it."

"What? No! I couldn't." I stammered.

"Yes, please take it. I have others. It will look beautiful on you."

I was speechless and a little embarrassed as if I had unconsciously asked for it.

As she put it in my hand, I managed, "Thank You, that's really so sweet and generous of you."

Leticia was smiling in joy. Her eyes had that Santa Claus twinkle that I love to see in people. Although I don't know her as a *friend*, I know in my heart she's a good, kind person. I've watched her with her grandchildren from my kitchen window while doing dishes. I've never heard her yell and although the children can get rambunctious while playing in the courtyard before it's time for baths and bed, you can see how much she truly loves and enjoys them. It always makes me smile to watch their interactions. She is the tender grandmother we all want to have in our lives.

But here's the question: Did Leticia know that I had two rather large skin cancers removed in the last few months, and my dermatologist was badgering me about wearing a wide-brimmed hat whenever I went outside? No. She didn't know that about me.

Did she know that my thirty-year-old son had slowly died of AIDS during those years when the doctors were unsuccessfully trying to find anything that would stop it or even slow it down? That during those three long years of his suffering, I had brought him fresh sunflowers every few visits. They made him so happy.

No, she didn't know that about me.

Did she know that we dropped sunflowers over the end of Malibu Pier every year on his yahrzeit, the day he died, and on his birthday? Did she know we sprinkled his ashes into the sea with sunflowers all those many years ago? No, she didn't know.

Did she know that my daughter and granddaughter bring me sunflower bouquets on special occasions and sometimes, just because? No, she didn't know that, either.

Leticia was just being generous and kind because that is her nature. That is who she is. She didn't know how that hat would touch me on so many levels. But isn't that the point? If we follow our instincts that are born of love, magic happens all around us, even when we don't know it.

Jeanne Zeeb-Schecter

A Timid Tiger and More True Tales

Competing in sports has a way of bringing out the best and the worst in all of us—the most ruthless, win-at-all-costs attitudes along with the very best aspects of self-improvement, coaching, teamwork and sportsmanship. And yes, even kindness. To generalize, sports competition is a mixed bag, but I have always made some peace with the disparate ingredients inside that bag. And I've been hopelessly addicted to several sports since even before...

...April 1968. I was eight-and-a-half years old, a third grader who was excited to play Little League baseball for the first time. 1968 was a transformative, disruptive year for America, and in some ways, for my family as well. My older brothers (Dan and Josh) and I all switched from attending a Jewish day school in Camden, New Jersey to going to Mount Laurel Township's public schools. Although we each knew a kid or two from the neighborhood, this was a big adjustment for each of us.

I made this transition in third grade, and now hold vague but fond memories of my first public school teacher, Mrs. Marshall. Although I can't tell you that I was Mr. Popular in third grade, schoolwork was easy, I made some friends and mostly looked forward to gym class and recess. But at times (in part due to being one of very few Jewish kids in my school) I felt like an outsider. As Spring approached, I approached my parents to sign me up for Little League baseball, which was run by the township's recreation program called Greentree. My parents agreed, and thus began a mostly enjoyable eight-year ride.

As inauspicious debuts go, however, mine was spectacular. One day shortly after we registered, my dad handed me the phone. A man who I'll call Mr. S introduced himself as the coach of the Phillies. (Our 8–10-year-old Phillies soon resembled the Philadelphia Phillies of that era: we lost more games than we won.) He welcomed me to the team and asked me if I could make our first practice on April 6. I said something to the effect of *Of course! Thank you!* To this day, I not only enjoy playing games, but even love practices. I was psyched for my very first practice. So far, so good.

When I gave my dad the news, his face sagged with disappointment. That wasn't like my usually supportive dad unless I had just screwed up in some way. I had.

"Matthew, didn't you tell Mr. S that April 6 is the date of Dan's Bar-Mitzvah?"

Allow me a historical note. The great Martin Luther King, Jr. was assassinated on April 4 of that year, just two days prior to my first prac, er, Dan's Bar-Mitzvah. Due to fears of rioting in the area, his Friday night service was canceled, but everything went well the next day, when Dan—per Jewish ritualistic tradition—became a man.

"Well...no, I didn't think of it. Sorry, Dad. Can you call him back?"

The call was made, and by the time Dad got off the phone with my coach, I found out that I would miss our other preseason practices due to the Jewish holiday of Passover. Three years prior to this, the legendary Sandy ("Left Arm of God") Koufax refused to pitch the opening game of the 1965 World Series as it fell on the solemn holiday of Yom Kippur. He was rightfully celebrated for his devotion to his religion. And me, the "right arm of a skinny eight-year-old?" Well, I was no Koufax and could've used all the practice time available.

When I showed up for our first game, I didn't know anyone on the team, and barely knew how to play. I started as one of those kids who the coaches were mandated to play the league minimum: two innings in the field (and hopefully, where there weren't any balls hit) and one time at-bat. Exactly two innings and one at-bat per game. That said, Coach S was a nice, patient man who seemed to be in coaching for the right reasons: to help kids learn how to play the game. His young son, however, had some serious control issues.

During that first game when I was relegated to the sideline for the first four innings, Mike S must have been plotting his move. Wham! Out of nowhere, he socked me in the eye with his baseball mitt. *Welcome to the show, kid!* And shortly after, I was welcomed almost as rudely by the opposing pitcher.

Not having played a real game of baseball before, I was the proverbial deer in the headlights as I stepped to home plate. Even worse: To my eyes, first base seemed to be more in line with home plate than the pitcher's rubber was. (There was no elevated pitcher's mound.) Two strikes zipped by me as I squinted at the first baseman. I finally spotted the pitcher. The correct focus didn't help me at all. The opposing pitcher threw some ten-year-old-kid gas, and I was completely overmatched. I swung about a full second after his heater popped the catcher's mitt. Strike three! Back to my bench, and within range once again of the coach's wild son.

The bleachers may have been even rougher. My staunchest fan and defender who answered then to *Mommy* was aghast that several parents were angry that I was allowed to play my two innings (and one disastrous plate appearance) even though I didn't attend team practices. Mom was right, but even though I still recall this calamitous debut, back then I moved on from it. I just wanted to fit in, and not get mocked by the other kids. Let alone the other parents.

I'm happy to report that my youth baseball experiences got much better. For one, how could things not improve? And reflecting on my eight years in Greentree baseball, the number of negative incidents were minimal, and more than offset by the good times. Most coaches were there for the right reasons and approached their volunteer commitments with enthusiasm and even a sense of kindness. And most parents were friendly and supportive.

A few memories stand out for me, even if they may make for unusual takes on the concept of kindness. During that third-grade season which included an assault to the eye and heckling from our own fans, I gradually became just a little more adept at baseball. I even played more than the minimum required two innings on occasion.

Enter our best player's slightly mysterious father, who seemed to take a liking to me. He was a tall, skinny guy with tattooed arms at a time when visible tattoos were about as common as a Jewish player on the Phillies. Mr. P had a prematurely raspy voice that suggested he lived life with a certain gusto. I envisioned him swinging off a ship—for want of a chandelier—and sporting a sailor's uniform while brandishing a sword. Something like that.

When I came to bat one time, I heard his by-then-familiar gruff voice, "Hey Tiger, come on Tiger, you can do it." I'm sure it made me smile then, just as its recollection does now. Soon, I even had a real batting average—not just .000. My parents would report that Mr. P would sometimes tell them, "Hey, that Matt is a real tiger out there." Truth be told, *Third Grade Me* was an awfully timid tiger, but the would-be-sailor's words—ironic or not—were motivational. Every time he would greet me as "Tiger", it would put a grin on my young, impressionable face, and help instill in me a greater sense of belonging and confidence. Thank you, Mr. P.

A surreal incident that took place three years later reflected a peculiar variety of kindness. By sixth grade, I was among the better players in my age group, and I started pitching that year with success. After one game when we won and I pitched and batted well, a teammate's dad (Mr. A) called me over. He shook my hand and placed a $5 bill in it. I was flabbergasted and elated. I envisioned all the sodas and Tastykakes (I was partial to *Koffee Kakes* and *Chocolate Juniors*) I could buy with a five-spot!

When I told my parents about it, my dad said that I couldn't accept his generosity.

I thought: Why not? Will I lose my amateur eligibility?

(Readers: I don't want you to get the mistaken impression that I became a superstar player. I was pretty good, loved to play sports, and enjoyed playing with my teammates. Oh, I still do, as I continue to engage in friendly battle in men's softball leagues. But three years after this *illegal payment*, I would try out for and get cut from my high school baseball team. Perspective can be a double-edged sword.)

My dad thought about it, telling me that five dollars was a lot of money, and that it would be an imposition on Mr. A if I accepted it. In the end as I recall, we decided that returning the gift may have caused Mr. A some embarrassment. I'm debating this conundrum as I type, but I would like to think that the kindness shown by both Mr. A and my parents clashed just a little, if for noble reasons. That said, the aftermath was wonderful: lots of Chocolate Juniors and Koffee Kakes!

A couple years later, I had the good fortune of playing in the 13-15-year-old division for a coach who I greatly enjoyed competing for. He was an ideal leader for what the league was—a decent brand of baseball for kids who were unlikely to ever suit up in Major League Baseball. He knew a thing or two about the game and wanted us to win, but never took the results too seriously. I don't remember him ever yelling at us, and he always exhibited a lot of confidence in me.

I played for Mr. C in both my 8th and 9th-grade years, and for the following year, the coaches held a draft. One evening, I received a phone call from Mr. C who told me that I was his first pick, choosing me over a younger (but in my mind) much better player who I'll name *Johnny Harper*. I was shocked to be chosen over Johnny and, in effect, questioned my coach's competence as a general manager. "You're a better player than he is" he said, supposedly with a straight face.

I might question my coach's judgment on player acquisitions, but not his kindness. Well, perhaps I was a better teammate than Johnny, and he recognized that.

My memory bank gives me access to this baseball scene that seems to substantiate this. I was pitching against the team that Johnny Harper played on. In the top of the first with two outs and nobody on base, Johnny pounded a long triple off me, and then the next batter—a friend from my neighborhood who was already a very promising high school player—stepped to the plate. He ripped a screamer up the middle that I caught out of a combination of self-preservation, quick reflexes and dumb luck. That ended the inning with no damage done on the scoreboard or to me.

Jogging off the *mound* to our bench, I must have had a huge smile on my face. Partly from relief and partly from just the enjoyment of playing and giving it my all. Harper, who was stranded on third, was a fierce competitor. I made what I thought was friendly eye contact with him, but he evidently took offense.

"What are you smiling about, Matty? You don't see *me* smiling."

I was a bit puzzled, as we had always been on friendly terms, but I also didn't want to say anything that might provoke him. Later, a thought hit me. I'll never consistently pound a baseball like Johnny can, but maybe my coach—recognizing another good soul—had made the right draft pick.

I started this piece with a bit of a truism: Competitive sports has a way of bringing out the best and the worst in all of us. Both teamwork and competition can elicit extreme behavior. At times, I've lost my temper (always at myself) during competitions, and usually there have been others who were there to calm me down. Sometimes, it's been the other way around, and I've played the part of a calming influence on them. Luckily, I have had good role models along the way to try to point me in the right direction.

When it comes to various sports and games, I wish I could act more consistently like my greatest role model in life. My dad of blessed memory, Robert J. Goldberg, brought his gentle, kind-hearted and appreciative nature to so many endeavors, including sports. Dad never got too carried away when either playing or watching a game. A good ping-pong player, he was delighted when after I tried to defeat him so many times over the years, I finally accomplished this elusive feat. (And yes, I desperately wanted to win, but once I did, I had profound mixed feelings about doing so.)

Dad loved playing chess, but at home he had no other takers. I'm sure it disappointed him that none of us took up his favorite game, but he never aggressively pushed it on us. He simply wanted us to learn the game and come to enjoy it because it brought him so much pleasure. Sure, he was never averse to winning a game (whether Scrabble, Monopoly, backgammon or cards), but his true joy came from simply spending time together. And he was genuinely happier when one of us, rather than he, won a family game.

This book was created to tell stories about the acts, words and feelings of kindness received from those other than family members and close friends. I beg your indulgence for taking a slight detour so I could share the example of my own dad.

Kind acts, words and feelings are rendered, spoken and expressed every day, even on sports battlefields, and I would like to sincerely thank all the children and adults who approach games and life in the same noble way that my dad did.

Matthew J. Goldberg

Contributors' Bios

Dr. Carl R. Ackerman is the recipient of a Presidential scholarship from President George H. W. Bush. He earned a PhD in European History at U.C. Berkeley. Having taught history for 37 years in Hawaii at the Punahou (President Barack Obama's school/5th-12th grades) and Iolani Schools in Honolulu, Carl also founded and developed the Clarence T. C. Ching Partnerships in Unlimited Educational Opportunities (PUEO) Program. He is a board member of the Atherton YMCA, Youth Service Hawaii, and Straub Hospital. Carl lives in Manoa Valley, Honolulu with his wife, Dr. Lyn Kajiwara Ackerman. His oldest daughter, Laura, is an assistant professor at Arizona State University, and his youngest daughter, Jennifer, is also at ASU as an undergraduate in the Barrett Honors College. Website: carlackermanbooks.com.

Lori Alan, actor/writer/producer, is perhaps best known for her award-winning voice-over work. She has played a long-running role as Pearl Krabs on the animated television series SpongeBob SquarePants. She also voiced Diane Simmons on Family Guy, the Invisible Woman on Fantastic Four, and The Boss in the Metal Gear video game series. She's proud to be a part of the Pixar Family, voicing characters in Wall-e, Monster's University, Inside Out and portraying Bonnie's Mom in Toy Story 3 & 4. Lori's on-camera roles include Will & Grace, Ray Donovan, Shameless, Loot with Maya Rudolph and as Young Larry's Mom on Curb Your Enthusiasm. On stage credits include The Pee-wee Herman Show, solo show Lori Alan: The Musical, and the award-winning musical, Reefer Madness. All things Lori, including her pilot, *Do The Voice*, can be seen at: lorialan.com.

Linda Alster Nelson is a former New York trial attorney, the lucky wife of Jonathan Nelson and a mother of two. She is a tennis, Beatles and kindness enthusiast, and resides in Westchester County, New York.

Azure is a scientist working in Boston dealing with the problems of the digital world and trying in her small way to make an impact in having a cleaner and greener world. An avid traveler and a follower of tennis, she enjoys forging relations with people during her travels and has a weak heart for animals.

Growing up, **Phoebe Bellagamba** (now a sophomore at a Cherry Hill, NJ high school) always had a knack for storytelling, but it wasn't until she became an avid reader in middle school that she started writing down the ideas that were in her head. As a high school freshman, she took a writer's workshop course so she could focus more on her skills of becoming a writer.

Susan Berin has written and produced TV shows for The Travel Channel, HGTV, E! Entertainment, SYFY, and more. Her essays from the perspective of a widowed mom who re-enters the dating scene have been published on medium.com and the Erma Bombeck Writer's Workshop. Susan has also spent the last several years as a volunteer at her daughters' schools, a local food pantry and homeless drop-in center. She currently volunteers at a city animal shelter and is in the process of starting a blog about her experiences there. She hopes her words will encourage the public to adopt from their local shelters. Susan resides in Los Angeles, CA.

Joe Berkery has been editor/writer for the Philadelphia Daily News and Inquirer since 1990. He has won numerous awards for headline writing, including national headline writer of the year for 2014 by the American Copy Editors Society. He lives in Cherry Hill, N.J., with his wife, two kids, and a third son who's getting famous as a Broadway drummer. Besides family, his biggest loves are the Phillies, Eagles, and Big 10 college wrestling.

Chuck Brodsky is a storytelling, songwriting, modern-day troubadour whose genuine warmth and quirky, finely-crafted songs touch hearts, funny bones, and a nerve or two. With irony and wit, his thirteen CDs celebrate the eccentric, holy, courageous, inspiring, and the beautiful, while poking fun at what needs poking. Chuck began performing around northern California in the late 1980s. Over the past 29 years he's played concerts all across the USA and in eleven countries. Several of his songs have appeared in movies and on tv, while others have been covered by artists as diverse as David Wilcox, Kathy Mattea, The African Children's Choir of Uganda, and Frogwings (with Warren Haynes and Derek Trucks). The National Baseball Hall of Fame, where he's performed three times, has dubbed him "Baseball's Troubadour Poet Laureate." Website: https://www.chuckbrodsky.com

Akita Brooks is a Certified Spiritual Life Coach, Stress Management Coach and Wellness Advocate, and supports emotionally sensitive individuals to creatively express themselves. Her wellness coaching and teaching practices include Aromatherapy, TranscenDance™ Facilitation, Ho'oponopono-Inspired Meditations, Mindful Art, EFT/TFT Tapping, and other Mind-Body clearing methodologies. She is the author of Full Glass Living: 28 Days to Dump Limiting Beliefs, which became Amazon's #1 New Release under Popular Psychology: Mental Illness. Akita enjoys exploring art, spending time with her family, geocaching with friend and playing with her cat Smokie Nova.
For more about Akita, visit www.fullglassliving.com or write to www.fullglassliving@gmail.com.

Mike Butler wears many hats but never actually wears hats! Born and raised in the Annapolis Valley, Nova Scotia, Mike has lived and worked in Wolfville for 20 years and has become a friendly face in his community. Since December 2009, Mike has been a part of 77 local community theatre productions, in the capacity of acting, directing, producing, marketing and stage managing. Mike was founder and operator of the Wolfville Theatre Collective and in 2020, leapt into the role of Councillor for the Town of Wolfville. In his spare time, Mike is an avid reader, writer and enjoys spending time with family, friends, and his amazing husband Ian! Mike can be reached at butlermike50@gmail.com

Ian Carlton is an industrial engineer who has worked in the corrugated container industry for over 40 years. Prior to that, he worked for Chrysler Corporation, which led to his love and collection of Chrysler muscle cars of the '60s and '70s. He began playing Little League baseball in 1966 and has played baseball and then softball continuously every year since then. Married 42 years, a father of two, and a grandfather of two, Ian considers himself to really be the luckiest man on the face of the earth. With all due respect to Lou Gehrig.

John T. Childress is an experienced business leader who excels at strengthening businesses to grow and increase revenue. He holds a Bachelor of Science in Finance from Rutgers University School of Business. John is certified in the Predictive Index, Balanced Scorecard, and Kauffman FastTrac tools and programs. At age 20, he became one of the first African American Franchisees in the 4,000-store Domino's Pizza chain. John was later selected to serve as Executive Director of the African American Chamber of Commerce in Philadelphia, then established Childress Business Consulting (www.ChildressBiz.com). In 2018, John joined Mosaic Development Partners as Director of Business Development. Mosaic has leased over 400,000 square feet of commercial space and built profitable, sustainable projects across the state of Pennsylvania.

Matt Clairmont is a father, husband, writer, baseball fan, and terrible singer from New Minas, Nova Scotia. He has written novels in several genres, numerous short plays, and a collection of poetry. In 2021, he published his first book in an adventure series for young readers, *Junior Alexander and the Balance of Power*. Since 2017 he has owned and operated Clairmont Publishing Services, a small business designed to help aspiring authors reach their publication goals.

Website: https://www.clairmontpublishing.com/

Elliot Dennis, a native of Brooklyn, NY, spent six years in the U.S. Naval Air Reserves, and worked 23 *wonderful* years for Eastman Kodak. Elliot has been an avid member of Toastmasters International, and has enjoyed 42 years as a member of Princeton (NJ) Toastmasters. In Toastmasters, he has been a District Governor, won numerous speech contests and received a citation from the international president for his work in getting others who stutter involved and learning effective speech techniques. Elliot resides in East Norriton, PA, and dotes on his seven *delicious* grandkids and three great grandkids.

Carol Diezel is the business manager for an animal hospital in southern New Jersey. A mother of three, and grandmother of 3, she spent her sophomore year of high school in Naples, Italy and her junior year summer in Brazil visiting family. Her passions include a love of travel and of animals, sewing (she's made several prom gowns) and wine tasting. Carol is in the process of creating a "wine shack" in her yard, and her youngest son went to school and earned his degree in fermentation sciences, and now *living the life* in Napa Valley. At the time of writing, she plans to visit Napa to meet her newest grandson.

Sheri S. Dollin is the Social Emotional Implementation Specialist for a K-8 school. She has decades of experience as an educator teaching people young and old, and more recently, as a mindfulness facilitator. She's played a key role as a champion for innovative projects bringing together stakeholders and building impactful programs in autism and education. Sheri is the co-author of *The FRIEND® Program*, an approach for individuals with autism and their peers in inclusive settings. When not working in schools, Sheri teaches mindfulness classes (www.sheridollin.com), writes about navigating her sister's unique illness and enjoys new adventures.

Cathy Dreyfuss was born in New York, raised in Los Angeles, and has lived on Venice Beach for the last 45 years. An attorney and social justice activist, she represented indigent defendants and immigrants in criminal courts from 1984 to 2022, when she decided to leave lawyering for a more creative life. She has been writing personal stories for several years and is currently working on a memoir.

Rachelle Elias is originally from the island of Key West, Florida. She is now a psychotherapist in private practice in Southern California, with a specialty in bereavement counseling, as well as marriage and family therapy. She has worked in community mental health, and as a counselor for the Staff of the Survivors of the Shoah Visual History Foundation, as they collected testimonies of Holocaust survivors. Her stories are gleaned from 40 years of professional experience, as well as her personal experience as a wife, mother, grandmother, and great-grandmother. Her major interests are travel, spirituality, art, and nurturing family and friendships. She can be reached at rachelleelias@gmail.com.

Sean Ewert tells his stories in Chicago and Los Angeles at such shows as The Moth (storySLAM Winner "Nostalgia" Los Angeles 2021), USA Today Storytellers Project (Western/Sunbelt and National shows), JAM Creative Stories, This Much Is True, Flick Lit, Bike Winter Chicago, Story Club Chicago, Story Salon, The ReBoot, The Laugh Factory, Pour One Out and The Antidote. When Sean is not on-stage telling stories, he coaches storytellers and leads personal narrative workshops. He works during the day at the Spondylitis Association of America, helping those living with the disease share their stories about being a pain warrior and elevating public awareness of spondyloarthritis. Sean lives with his partner John and rescue dog, Pilot.

Anna Factor is a physical therapist, and a yoga teacher. She completed her 21-week yoga teacher training designed by Sadhguru, in India. Personal development is one of her passions and she enjoys assisting individuals seeking new and wider perspectives. ("Remembering our own power is magical".) She can be reached at: shifttopositive@gmail.com. You can also check her out at www.consciousplay.us.

Marla Feldman is a teacher, writer, blogger, and online mompreneur. Her work has previously appeared in Susan Heim's Twice the Love: Stories of Inspiration for Families with Twins, Multiples and Singletons, and Chicken Soup for the Soul, It's Twins!. Marla lives in New Jersey with her husband of 35 years and is a mother of three adult children. In her free time, she likes to bake, read, and volunteer.

Julia Field-Mitchell lives in North Booval - Ipswich, Queensland (Australia) with her daughter, who she also provides care for. Her hobbies include being with her pets, which include three parrots and two great Danes plus an ACS sausage dog. Julia enjoys riding her electric scooter with her girl riding her bike, birds in the basket and the dogs also in tow.

Rhonda Fink-Whitman, the author of *94 Maidens, Mrs. Graceland,* and the graphic novel–*Daughters of the Holocaust*–is also a wife, mother, daughter and granddaughter of Holocaust survivors, a former radio and TV personality, educator, speaker, and creator of *The Mandate Video* on YouTube. Her political advocacy helps states enact bills that require Holocaust education. Learn more and find the free downloadable teacher's guide for *94 Maidens* at www.94maidens.com. The author's books are available on Amazon in paperback and Kindle. Search *94 Maidens* on YouTube for classroom-friendly interviews with Holocaust survivors and WWII heroes. Like *94 Maidens* on Facebook and follow on Twitter, too.

Meredith Flynn, a former health care executive, is a writer, actor, world traveler, photographer and avid mah-jongg player. She's a hospice volunteer and also mentors teenage girls through the LA-based organization *Write Girl*.

Lauri Fraser is an American voice actress who has spent more than 20 years lending her talents to animation projects spanning film, TV series, commercials and video games. Lauri's vocal variations can be heard as: Marie Antoinette ("Peabody and Sherman); Mrs. Olson ("Olaf's Frozen Adventure,"); both Rocky and Natasha ("The Adventures of Rocky and Bullwinkle'); and "Rocky J. Squirrel" (Geico Insurance). When not in a recording booth, Lauri can be found performing stories at venues in and around Hollywood. She produced her own acclaimed live storytelling series and podcast, "I Love A Good Story," for eleven years. But she's most proud of her performance as herself on the mega-hit ABC television series "Shark Tank." Lauri and her sister pitched their father's invention, *Hugo's Amazing Tape*--and got a deal!

Born in Mexico in 1972, **Antonio Gandía** is a bassist, composer, producer, music teacher and a graduate from Berklee College of Music. He has played with Antonio Sánchez, Miguel Zenón, Alex Mercado, Oriente López and Diego Maroto, among others. A former columnist for the Músico Pro Magazine for 6 years. Antonio is a member of ASCAP and his compositions have been used in American TV programs. He has participated in many recordings, two of which were nominated for a Latin Grammy Award. Currently, Antonio teaches music in South New Jersey, where he lives with his wife and three sons.

Jeremy Garson is chief of staff at a nonprofit called the Bridge Alliance (www.BridgeAlliance.us), which is dedicated to helping America live up to its potential. He and his wife Stacy met while Jeremy was studying at the University of Michigan Law School, where Jeremy became a diehard Wolverines fan. After living together in D.C. for a few years, they moved to Stacy's hometown of Cherry Hill–down the street from Stacy's parents and close to Jeremy's parents and his hometown in the Philadelphia suburbs. When he isn't working his day job, Jeremy enjoys umpiring, shooting around at the local basketball court, and holding onto the Philadelphia Eagles' 2018 Super Bowl win for eternity.

Laurie Ginsburg is a writer, dancer and foodist, as well as a circle sorceress and community alchemist. She provides integrative bodywork and health education, using body/mind modalities, and offers individual and group counseling and deep fun adventures. Her motto is ""Be the Festival you want to see in the world!" For more information, visit laurieginsburg.com.

Rich Glass lives in South Jersey and is married with two adult children. His interests include supporting the Philadelphia sports teams, going to concerts and doing genealogy research where he has found dozens of new cousins that until recently, he never knew existed.

Linda Goldman, a native Los Angeleno, was first published in the June, 1952 issue of Parent Teacher News with a piece entitled "Silk Story", about the life cycle of silkworms. She didn't attempt to write again until 2014, since her life was full (in this exact order) with partying, marriage, parenting, working, and (late in the game) studying. She received her B.A. degree in Sociocultural Anthropology at UCLA which led, in a story too long to tell here, to a gratifying career as a dispute resolution professional. Her primary interest has always been humans – what separates us and what binds us together. She is proud to be part of this life-affirming book titled *Rings of Kindness*.

Scott Goldman is a Realtor™, music buff and baseball historian residing in Westchester County New York. He has always been an advocate for equality, tolerance, kinship, placidity and kindness. Now, more than ever we need to find the ties that bind as opposed to those which divide.

William H. Graham III grew up near Clementon Lake in Southern New Jersey. As a small boy, he puzzled over why his grandfather would take him fishing, but never bother to put more than a small brass washer on the end of his line ("a worm would catch a fish…and then I'd have a reason to leave this lovely lake"). William now makes his home in the splendorous Rocky Mountains of Colorado, where he enjoys woodworking and fly fishing with brass washers…

Eric C. Gray is originally from Plainview, New York, and earned his Bachelor of Arts from SUNY New Paltz. In 1974, he came to San Francisco and a 40-year career with the Department of Labor. He is married to Lynn, has two kids and a granddaughter, Juliet. Eric has written two books of folks' personal baseball memories from around the world, *Bases to Bleachers* and *Backyards to Ballparks*. He is working on a book of concert memories. If you have stories, or want the book, the website is basestobleachers.com or contact him at eric.baseballstories@gmail.com

Lisa Hamm-Greenawalt is a former Associated Press journalist and communications consultant. After stepping off the breadwinning treadmill, she chose to become a nomadic retiree, splitting her time between a lake chalet in Vermont in summer and a house near the ocean in Puerto Rico in winter, while traveling in spring and fall. She always has a cat by her side, and a couple of kids when they visit from college. She has written a novel and a children's book, and maintains a travel blog/vlog called Messy Suitcase (messysuitcase.com) with her husband and co-adventurer, Bob Greenawalt. When not birdwatching, hiking, cycling, snorkeling, or making music, she can be found in front of her laptop, cat in lap, working on her next book idea.

Wendy Hammers is a hard core hyphenate - actor/writer/stand up comic/writing coach/live events producer/podcast host, and author. Acting: Curb Your Enthusiasm, The Sopranos, Mad About You. Onstage: National tour of Old Jews Telling Jokes. As a comic, she's been featured on Oprah. As an author, her published work includes: What Was I Thinking: 58 Bad Boyfriend Stories (St. Martins Press) and tousmesregimes.com. (Marabout Press) As a keynote speaker, Ms. Hammers travels the country and speaks about her most impressive credit to date, the fact that she is a seven + years Pancreatic Cancer survivor. She lives and thrives in Los Angeles, CA, with her husband Garth and her son Griffin. You can learn more, connect with Wendy, and listen to the Tasty Words podcast here: wendyhammers.com. @WendyJoysWorld on Instagram

Ellen Heuer is an award-winning Foley artist, writer and sometimes comedian. With over 300 Foley credits to her name, she is considered world-renowned for her work, that includes everything from *Showgirls* to *Schindler's List* to *The Incredibles* to *12 Years A Slave*. She lives and thrives in Los Angeles, California and can occasionally be seen on stage at The Comedy Store, making light of the world.

Pat Kelly is a retired learning and development consultant. During her career, she developed, managed and conducted various training programs and facilitated learning events for leaders and employees for multiple organizations across the United States. She currently lives in New Jersey with her husband of 43 years and has been blessed with three children and two grandchildren. Her passions include hiking, traveling, spending time at her camper at the beach and hanging out with family.

Richard Kouhoupt is an accountant and certified financial planner who has been in the tax practice since 1985 with Wells Fargo Bank and has held various titles including Tax Team Leader, Vice President and Senior Fiduciary Tax Analyst. Rich enjoys gardening, Toastmasters, church, community outreach, playing piano and singing. He also is a traditionalist and believes in honesty, integrity and values learned from past generations.

Steve Levin briefly worked for NRDI before becoming a laboratory manager at Temple University in the microbiology/immunology department for 11 years. Holding advanced degrees in biology and education, Steve was an honored biology educator for 18 years at Nottingham North High School (NJ) and also served as an adjunct professor at St. Joseph's (PA) University. He has won more than a dozen competitive grants for lesson plans, and has been filmed twice by *New Jersey Classroom Close Up:* the first in 2007-2008 (search under *Whodunnit*) won an Emmy award; the second, *Science Geek* (2018) was nominated for an *Emmy.*

Donna McCart Welser retired from business and information technology management, after an amazing, thirty-two-year long career working for UnitedHealth Group, Optum. She then pursued a master's in labor and employment relations at Rutgers University, NJ while also writing her first book, *Rue's Butterfly,* that chronicles her journey caring for her terminally ill husband and then reinvestment in life as a young widow. Donna considers herself an adventurer, *apocaloptomist* (hopes for the best, prepares for the worst), and world warrior focused on living her bucket list. She and her husband Mark, also previously widowed, took the plunge and married during the Covid pandemic, blending their family of two cats, three dogs, and a full tank of fish in addition to their two daughters, son, and extended families.

Jim McGrath lives with his wife Debbie and their two cats in the hinterlands outside of Raleigh, NC. Well, actually three cats, one is being cat-sat while his daughter is overseas for an extended bit. Because it was Matt who asked Jim if he had a story for publication, Jim knew he'd have to step up his writing game, as best as he could! Jim enjoys the occasional glass of Malbec, trips to Virginia International Raceway, and is a huge fan of Formula 1 racing along with the 24 Heures du Mans and other various forms of motorsport. He also holds the amateur radio callsign - W2PAU - see you on the bands! Email: jim@mcgrathfamily.org

Svetlana Mellein started writing during the 2020 election, "the first one I got to vote in after 18 years of living in this country. I often keep my thoughts and opinions to myself and feel much more comfortable listening or observing. When writing, my number one goal is authenticity without holding back, which is terrifying. And my golden rule is to feel something strong inside in order to write a piece. You can find more of my short stories on https://onebody.medium.com/ ."

Stefani Milan is the author of *The Kolney Hatch Series* (under R.A. Milan), *The Rescue Cat Series* (under Stefani Milan), and *This Side of the Dream: A Memoir*. She received her B.A. in English from Rutgers University Camden. In addition to writing, she is certified in Nutrition and Healthy Living from Cornell University. She has been a licensed esthetician for over 15 years and is currently finishing her certification through the Chopra Center as a Chopra Health Instructor. She continues to write and teaches healthy living and well-being in South Jersey, where she lives with her husband, son, dog, and rescued cats. Her website is www.stefanimilan.com.

Nate Miller (in his own words): "Baseball is my game! I've loved it since I was a kid. The sights, sounds, smells, and strategy... I love it all! I'm from Arlington, TX, and I couldn't be prouder of it! I'm a huge Texas Rangers guy! I've been following them for nearly a decade. I have an Associate of Applied Science Degree in Radio Broadcasting from Brown College in Mendota Heights, MN, and a Bachelor of Science Degree in Sports Marketing & Media from Full Sail University in Winter Park, FL. I have a real passion for sports, and I currently cover the Rangers as a beat writer for www.lastwordonbaseball.com."

Deanna Neil is the award-winning author of *The Land of Curiosities*, a young adult, historical-fiction trilogy about Yellowstone. She also penned *Time for Parks*, an illustrated children's book. Her books garnered 12 awards including a Benjamin Franklin, Moonbeam Children's Book Award, and the 2015 Living Now Evergreen Medal, commemorating "world-changing books published since the year 2000." Her play *Fracturing*, an adaptation of Ibsen's *Enemy of the People*, was produced and workshopped across the country. As a journalist, Neil worked for the Air America Radio network, NPR, KCET and blogged for the *Huffington Post*. An accomplished musician and performer, you can sometimes catch her singing along with her ukulele. She is also a prominent educator and service officiant in the Jewish community. www.innovativejudaism.com

Akweli Parker is a writer based in southern New Jersey. He has worked as a janitor, a journalist, a speechwriter to the C-suite and an investment industry professional, among other occupations. His number one passion is sustainable travel, through which he has helped with cheetah conservation in South Africa, elephant preservation in Thailand and protecting natural ecosystems in many other countries. His other areas of interest and expertise include blockchain, finance, and the global transition to renewable energy. When not researching or writing about these topics (or traveling), he can often be found hiking in the city, countryside, or mountains. He's a strong—some say fanatical—believer in the power of simply walking to unleash creativity and overall well-being. Contact him at Linkedin.com/in/akweliparker

Jackson Phillips is a full-stack developer who leads a team of multi-national developers for an industry-leading consulting firm. He resides in the greater New York City area with his wife, two sons, and two daughters. In his free time, Jackson enjoys spending weekends boating and fishing with his family, playing basketball, and building model cars.

Mark Pinzur taught math in the Cherry Hill, NJ high schools for 35 years before working at a charter school in Camden and the Doane Academy in Burlington. He lives with his wife Maxine and cat Molasses in Cherry Hill. Although his daughter lives in Seattle and his son and daughter-in-law are in London, he tries not to take this as a commentary on his parenting. His interests are singing, word puzzles and tennis, not necessarily in that order.

Richard Plinke graduated with high honors from Rutgers University with a BA in English Literature before embarking on a successful 35-year career in media sales. He has written three critically acclaimed books—*From the Jaws of the Dragon: Sales Tales and Other Marginally Related Stuff, More Droppings from the Dragon: A Hitchhiker's Guide to Sales* and *Dancing in the Cave of the Dragon: Adventures in the Wonderland of Sales,* plus numerous articles and columns on the art of selling. In 2020, he published a satirical book on the stay-at-home orders called *COVID 19 House Arrest.* He is currently working on his first work of fiction, *The Capricious Nature of Being,* a collection of short stories.

John Rosengren is an award-winning freelance journalist based in Minneapolis whose articles have appeared in the Atavist, the Atlantic, GQ, the New Yorker, Sports Illustrated, and the Washington Post Magazine, among other publications. He has published ten books, including the novel "A Clean Heart," a loosely autobiographical story about a young man working in a treatment center run by a hard-drinking nun with an MBA. You can see some of John's work at www.johnrosengren.net

Scott Russell, a native of the Bronx, New York resides in "The Cliffs" of North Attleboro, Massachusetts with Peg, his long-suffering bride of 37 years and their assorted deranged felines. Scott is a baseball lover, absolutely adores animals of all kinds and actively opposes anything that serves to divide us. His previous book titles include *Joey, Prophet's End, The Scorekeeper,* and two books (so far) in his series with former Major League Baseball pitcher Bill Lee: *The Spaceman Chronicles* and *The Final Odyssey of The Sweet Ride - Bill "Spaceman" Lee's Epic Journey Through America.*

Luz Sanchez is a filmmaker, author, speaker, and generational breaker. She is from Mexico City and lives in Los Angeles CA. She Graduated with a BA in Cinema and TV Arts. Luz is a DTM (Distinguished Toastmaster). She collaborated on two books, *Life Boosts* and *Women Who Rock 2*, and is the sole author of the e-book *Stolen Identity: What to do when it happens to you.* Luz was also once crowned Ms. Elite Mexico-America at the Woman of Achievement Pageant. Website: luz-sanchez.com

Dee-Dee Sberlo is a San Francisco native, mother of four, a writer, and a community organizer. She is currently collecting stories from women for her book about mothers, aunts and grandmothers who have influenced our lives in both positive and negative ways. She'd love to hear from you at: dyingtohearyourstories@gmail.com.

Deborah Schizer Scott teaches in the First Year Writing Program at Rowan University. She earned a Ph.D. in English from the University of Pennsylvania. In addition, Deborah tutors high school English, SAT prep (verbal sections only) and college application essays. You can find her online at www.theenglishclinicnj.com and www.facebook.com/EnglishClinicTutoring. Deborah loves personal writing, which she studied at the University of Pennsylvania. She is developing a couple of angles for a memoir, focusing on the repercussions of childhood illness as well as a journey through infertility and adoption. Deborah lives in Cherry Hill, New Jersey, with her husband and son.

Karen Schober is a renowned romance and fiction writer. Her books include the *Fire and Ice Series* and *Second Chance: A New Star*, plus several short stories under her pen name Karen Maneely. She is also the founder of Fireball Studio, a company that offers author consultations through the entire writing and publishing process and multi-media productions such as her weekly podcast, *The Author's Lighthouse*, aimed at new authors navigating the choppy waters of publishing. Karen has earned a B.A. in Psychology and an MBA with a focus on marketing.

Laurie Schur is a psychotherapist for 40+ years, and a documentary filmmaker with one documentary project called *The Beauty of Aging*. The films in this project explore myths about aging with stories of active, extraordinary American women over 80. Laurie says, "In these later years I have taken up writing as well, or as I like to say it, I'm in the writing phase of my life. I'm also an activist for many years and many causes. I'm currently doing pro bono work for people in Ukraine. I'm happily married, and close to my children and 4 grandchildren."
Website: www.beautyofaging.com
Contact: laurie.schur@gmail.com

Alicia Sedwick has Southern roots and California branches. She is a writer, actor, producer, professor, and strategic researcher for an international investigative firm. She was co-producer of LA's live storytelling event *Spark Off Rose* for fifteen years and currently teaches at UCLA's Theatre, Film and Television Department. She is also a speech/story coach and editor and most recently worked with a non-profit accelerator, supporting female tech entrepreneurs. Alicia holds an MFA from San Francisco's American Conservatory Theatre. Her play *Bringin' Home the Girl* was produced in NYC at HERE Space, and in LA at STAGES. More about her work at aliciasedwick.com

Linda Shaffer is an artist and writer living in Los Angeles, California. She is the author and illustrator of a children's book entitled *Mandy & Mew-Chi*, the story of a lonely little girl and a stray cat who form a friendship by learning to surf together. It is available at Amazon. Linda is currently in the middle of writing a novel set in Charleston, South Carolina where she lived for many years before moving to Los Angeles.

Josh Stehle is an author and autism advocate from Philadelphia, Pennsylvania. His global autism awareness brand, The Stehle Bros, has received millions of views on TikTok and has been featured on ABC News, The Art of Autism, The Ausome Show, and several other national media outlets (@thestehle.bros). Josh's debut book, *I am a Superhero Expert*, is a look at autism from a new perspective. It describes the unique experience of growing up with an autistic older brother, while providing a glimpse into the challenges that autistic people often face, highlighting the indescribable beauty that autism can bring to siblings through the shared experience of two brothers. *I am a Superhero Expert* releases on January 19th, 2023. Preorder *I am a Superhero Expert* today at www.joshstehle.com

Katie Sullivan is a high school sophomore in Cherry Hill, New Jersey, who lives with her parents, brother, and two dogs. She has written for her school's virtual newspaper, but this is her first published (printed) piece.

Lauren Sullivan is the Digital and Social Media Director at Sam Brown Healthcare Agency. Prior to joining the healthcare world, Lauren worked in broadcast and digital media for 18 years. She was the Director of Digital Content for CBS's eight owned and operated TV and radio stations in Philadelphia for nearly a decade spearheading all online efforts for talent, news, promotions, production, and sales. She is an animal lover and volunteer with Brookline Lab Rescue and the Animal Adoption Center in Lindenwold, NJ, as well as a board member for Complete Care Health Foundation, helping provide access to healthcare to anyone who needs it in Cumberland, Salem, Gloucester and Cape May County, NJ.

Mitchell Tiger currently resides in Peru. He has been blessed by surrounding love from immediate and extended family. Full appreciation of life allows complete enjoyment of experiences and friendships.

Dr. Peter Titlebaum is a professor at the University of Dayton. His areas of expertise include marketing, sales, fund-raising, activation, return on investment and return of objective strategies.

Born on St. Croix, **Cassandra Ulrich** allowed her imagination and daydreams to flourish. She has published *A Beautiful Girl, Love's Intensity, Billiard Buddies, Adelle and Brandon: Friends for Life, Zale's Tale* (short story in Beach Life), *Battle at Kitee* (Mad Scientist Sci Fi Writing Contest semi-finalist, a short story), *If It Kills Me, Danny R.O.S.S., Just Between Us* (a Black American Romance), and four poetic compilations. In 2021, two non-fiction stories got into Chicken Soup for the Soul's *I'm Speaking Now* and *Tough Times Won't Last But Tough People Will*. She is also a Do What's Write Writer's Group & Podcast co-host. http://mobile.cassandraulrich.com/, https://www.amazon.com/Cassandra-Ulrich/e/B008H7H6SW,

Retired teacher **Rebecka Vigus** is an author, speaker, and coach. Ms. Vigus has been writing since she was ten when a teacher told her, with her imagination he would see her in books one day. She believed him and started writing then. She loves spending time with family and friends. She uses her leisure time to crochet, swim, hike, and travel. She lives in her forever home in Nancy,

Kentucky amid the wildlife, cattle, dogs, and horses. Find her at https://www.rebeckavigus.com

Boliang Wang was born and raised in China. He came to the U.S. in 2014 and received the name Michael from his English teacher. Since then, he has been using Michael instead of his real name for eight years. He spent two years learning English and went to a community college after that. Then, he got his A.A. and B.A. degrees, and he is currently pursuing his MFA in Film. It's been a unique journey for him.

Born in Charleston, SC, formed in Raleigh, NC and reborn in Southern California, **Suzanne Weerts's** creative nonfiction essays can be found in *The Sun, Good Old Days Magazine,* in the recent anthology *The Pandemic Midlife Crisis: GenX Women on the Brink* and on numerous websites. Suzanne is a regular on storytelling stages across Southern California and directs and produces her own storytelling shows for local charities through jamcreativestories.com. She is currently working on a memoir based on her childhood in the south in the 1970s.

Ali Wolf can frequently be found writing, running, or being invigorated by the ocean. But she's most often in her kitchen, drinking coffee, baking, or dancing, making happy messes and memories with any combination of her seven children, two daughters-in-law, two sons-in-law, five grandchildren, or assorted fur family (currently at 2 dogs and 5 cats). "Just A Dad" is dedicated to the kindest woman she knows, the extraordinary Marilyn Ross.

Damaris Zayas is an avid book reader, writer, teacher and business owner. She finds inspiration in the everyday moments. She loves to spend her time reading, spending time with her dog Mya, family and friends.
Website:https://virtualexpertservice.com.
Connect: https://www.instagram.com/damariszay/

Jeanne Zeeb-Schechter, recently retired, has been a homeopathic doctor for 28 years and served as the chairperson and teacher at the American University of Complimentary Medicine for 20 years. She belongs to a writing class ("led by the brilliant Wendy Hammers") and teaches a Life Writing class. Jeanne is a member of Story Circle Network, a national women's writing group, and has been published in three of their anthologies, with poems in their quarterly magazine. Currently, she's writing a nonfiction book on using homeopathy and flower essences in the treatment of grief as well as a historical novel about a Celtic healer in the Appalachian Mountains. She is blessed to be married to a wonderful man, has a daughter, four granddaughters and eight great grandchildren.

Isabella Zhang is a junior at Cherry Hill High School East and loves the humanities and the arts, especially literature. She enjoys reading books, though mostly fiction and classics for the stories and flowery language, and among her favorite writers are Erin Morgenstern and Oscar Wilde.

About the Author

Matthew J. Goldberg is an inspirational humorist (writer, editor, speaker and coach) from the Philadelphia area—Cherry Hill, NJ, to be more precise—who communicates with both clarity and hilarity. That is a rarity. A part-time educator and tutor with a varied background in social services, sales and communications, Matt has authored six books, and has also helped other authors get their ideas and words into print.

His previous book titles include *Hot Ice Cream: Inspiring Life Lessons from Our Children*; *Wordapodia, Volume One: An Encyclopedia of Real Fake Words*; and *(co-author of) A Snowball's Chance: Philly Fires Back Against the National Media*. In addition to books, he has published hundreds of articles ranging from communication advice to sports to just about everything, mostly looking for ways to unite and entertain his readers. As a ghostwriter *(don't tell anyone)* and also in his own name, he has also written and published a zillion song parodies and poems.

Matt's favorite activities include playing softball, tennis and ping-pong; chilling out by reading or watching films; contributing time as a volunteer; and, especially, spending time with his family and friends.

For more information: matthewjgoldberg.com
Contact: matt@matthewjgoldberg.com

Stay in Touch

Thank you for reading *Rings of Kindness*. I hope that the stories resonated with you, and that you found them uplifting. I invite you to stay in touch with me for any of the following reasons:

> ➤ Tell me about your favorite stories, or maybe, you would like to share your own true story of kindness received from someone you weren't closely connected with at that time—for a possible second edition.

> ➤ Contact me to order personalized copies of *Rings of Kindness* for yourself or as gifts for birthdays, holidays (Mother's Day, Father's Day, Thanksgiving, Winter holidays, Valentine's Day...) and other occasions (or simply to spread the kindness to others).

> ➤ To order books for your organization, book club, school, care setting, etc.

> ➤ To schedule me as a speaker for your organization, or for a radio, TV or podcast appearance.

For more information: matthewjgoldberg.com
Contact: matt@matthewjgoldberg.com

Made in the USA
Middletown, DE
21 November 2022

15639258R00215